KINGS, GODS AND PEOPLE

Essays on Cultural History of Medieval Āndhradēśa

KINGS, GODS AND PEOPLE

Essays on Cultural History of Medieval Āndhradēśa

Prof. Krishna Kumari Myneni
Department of History and Archaeology,
Andhra University, Visakhapatnam

2004

Kaveri Books

New Delhi - 110 002

First Published in 2004

ISBN 81-7479-067-5

Published by : **Rakesh Goel**
Kaveri Books
4697/5-21A, Ansari Road
New Delhi-110002 (India)
Tel.: 2328 8140, 2324 5799
E-mail: kaveribooks@vsnl.com

Laser Typesetting by : Aarati Computers, Delhi-110 009

Printed at : Chawla Offset Printers, Delhi-110 052

PRINTED IN INDIA

This book is dedicated

to

my beloved parents:

Dr Myneni Sitaramaiah
&
Myneni Sarojini

PREFACE

This book is principally a study of the different less known aspects of the cultural history of the Andhras of the medieval times. It includes 17 essays analysed in four sections, which are either discussed at various academic gatherings or published elsewhere, and which relate mostly to the popular traditions, customs, practices, religious beliefs and ideology of the Andhras. The topics included in the volume were neither sufficiently focused nor discussed earlier in the works on the history and culture of the period and region. The textual traditions on the beliefs and customs of the common people who form the bulk of the population form the subject matter of the book. Since scholars have paid little attention to the seamy side of the socio-cultural life of the people, particularly to the aspects like robbery, alcoholism, famines and its aftermath, I have made an attempt to collect all the available historical evidences and analyse them through different approaches. The principal objective of this volume is to present how important the study of the cultural history of the common people in relation to the sacred centers and royalty is to gain a better understanding of the history of medieval Andhra. One of my concerns in this volume has been the analysis of the archaeological and historical sources with an inter-disciplinary approach and to examine the desirability of different concepts and models. Throughout this book I have shown how vital such interdisciplinary approach can be for analyzing the data on popular traditions, culture and religious ideology. Not only that, new facets of the cultural history of the past have been brought to light through these studies but these can also be a source of generating new questions for further research and encourage more scholars to take up their studies in new areas of research.

I express my grateful thanks to all the scholars and historians of Andhra who encouraged me to take up certain new themes and topics for my research from time to time, as well as for their invaluable suggestions and comments on my papers. I am grateful to Prof. Karel Vankooji, Leiden University, Leiden for his writings on art and iconography, which are a source of inspiration for me. I express my sense of gratitude and offer my respectful thanks to Dr Janice Stargardt, Sidney Sussex College, Cambridge for the academic support extended to me. I am extremely grateful to Dr (Mrs) Haripriya Rangarajan who organized a National Seminar on Tantrism at Hyderabad and encouraged me to participate in its deliberations. With her encouragement I could work on this theme and interact with both the academicians and tantric practitioners of our country.

It is my pleasant duty to record my thanks to my friends, well-wishers and members of the family who envinced keen interest in all my academic pursuits and encouraged me to keep writing.

I thank the publishers of the book for undertaking my work and presenting this volume to the academic world in a very attractive manner.

Myneni Krishna Kumari

CONTENTS

Section III
Art and Iconography

Section IV
Royalty, Women and Society

List of Plates

Chapter-11

INTRODUCTION

The medieval history of Andhra is noted for the abundance of data in the form of both archaeological and literary sources. The period that commences with the onset of the rule of the Chalukyas of Vengi to that of the end of Vijayanagra period is generally considered as the medieval period in Andhra history from the socio-economic and political considerations. The abundance of the stone inscriptions in Andhra in Telugu, Sanskrit, Tamil, Kannada and Oriya speak of the political as well as the cultural significance attached to some of its sacred and political centres as the places that attracted the attention of the people from different regions and places. The inscriptions that provide genuine and authentic information about the various aspects of political, socio-economic and cultural history are in large number when compared to those of the earlier periods. The several icons carved either within or outside Andhra in different iconographical forms not only reflect the religious ideology and faith of the people but also provide some idea about the changes in the history of religion and its demonstration through images. Besides these archaeological sources the literary works composed during the period form the flesh and blood of the historical data and help in filling the gaps in the understanding of the cultural history of Āndhradēśa. The different types of sources provide the historians not merely with substantial information on which they could base historical generalizations but also allow the application of a variety of relatively new tools of research such as psychohistorical analysis of the data as well as a range of historical interpretations particularly relating to the faiths, beliefs, customs, folklore traditions, popular traditions, tantric practices, religious symbolism of the icons, the king as the protector of land and people, and the role of the temples both as ritual and socio-cultural centres. The richness of the source material of Andhra though it suffers from some limitations did not draw much attention from the historians of East and West who showed a greater interest in the South Indian history, particularly in the regional histories of Tamilnadu and Karnataka than the history of Andhra.

The oral traditions, folk aesthetic expressions and local cultural practices reveal the diversity of Andhra region. The inter-relationship between royalty, religion and people encompasses a political, social, psychological and economic dimension making the life course an integral part rather than divisive and segmental. To reconstruct the cultural history, it is essential to understand the textual-historical as well as oral contextual sources. Generally, the historical sources focus on the royalty-feudalistic order and linkages of administration while the oral traditions describe and depict a meaningful picture of the cultural traditions of the people that cannot easily be gained through the written texts. A careful analysis of all these sources will help in knowing the linkages between the royalty, gods and the people of the society.

Some of the topics included in the work have long been the subject of interest and debates which have acquired importance more recently. Especially, the studies on Tantrism that include *tantra, mantra* and *yantra* had emerged as an essential of any religious system. Special doctrines and rituals are found in certain forms of religious systems to incorporate *tantra* in them. *Tantra* is such a method which regards life as real and believes that men have legitimate powers and potentialities. Studies on the tantric temples of the past and present demonstrate the architectural plan of the temple that incorporates the essentials of tantrism especially those of *Ṣaṭ chakrabhēda*.

Subjecting the historical sources to the psychohistorical analysis has brought to light some new insights into the cultural history of the Andhra region. The concern of the State and the temple management for the people in times of calamities like famines and the changed outlook of the people towards kingship are some of the important issues discussed in the work. Social evils like robbery and alcoholism on which no full-length studies have been done so far, are attempted for the first time to focus on the dark side of the social and cultural life of the people.

Appreciation of art and iconographical forms of gods and goddesses, besides focusing on its inner meanings and religious symbolism, is attempted to study the icons which are being exhibited in the museums outside the country. These studies demonstrate broadly the changes in the religious ideology of the people that are shown through the carving of a new type of iconographical forms that had an indirect bearing on the cultural history of Andhra.

SECTION - I
FOLKLORE AND PSYCHOHISTORY

1

Psychohistorical Approach to Popular Child Rearing Practices in Andhra

The main thrust of psychohistory is the study of people's mentality and the interest of the psycho-historians is to underline the inner life of the people with major emphasis on the socio-cultural aspects of society. With an aim to reconstruct the total history, attempts are being made by the historians of Annales school of thought to study the inner life of the people. As a result of the efforts made by the "new histories", there was a new appreciation of the radical possibilities of unconventional, more or less un-organised groups up till now being "hidden from history" now "becoming visible".[1] Social and cultural history suddenly emerged as a dominant historical concern and the study of "popular culture" came to be recognized as one of its central pre-occupation. Popular culture is the interface between folklore and elite culture. It is one aspect of post modernism shown on vertical scale, with the elite culture and folk culture occupying 10% of the top and the lowest slot respectively and the large middle slot of 80% occupied by popular culture.[2] Studies conducted earlier have revealed that these sections are not watertight compartments but there is on-going interaction among them. Popular culture is seen as a description of a particular way of life of the people, which expresses certain meanings and values not only in art and learning but also in institutions and ordinary behaviour.[3] An attempt has been made to probe into the child-rearing practices followed in medieval Andhra on the basis of folklore traditions including songs, ballads, folk tales, fable tales, children's rhymes, action songs, proverbs and riddles. It is also aimed at making a psycho-historical analysis of the child caring practices, the role of mother and father, their relations with their children in the process of bringing them up and to compare the distinct approach of the Andhra mother with that of the West. It also focuses on the impact of the closeness of the mother with her children on the personality development of the children.

Popular culture has been defined by Dai Smith as the description and analysis of the popular tasks, customs, folk beliefs, manners and entertainment within any given social order.[4] In order to gain a basic insight into the popular traditions, customs, rituals and religious traditions, we need to specify the social context and types of society. Here the distinction may be mentioned between "popular" and "popularized" i.e., between the notion of a popular culture and that of a popularized culture before dealing with the subject of the Hindu child-rearing practices in Andhra region. A careful examination of these two reveals not only the differences between popular culture and popularized culture but also their similarities. While popular culture indicates an implicit state or condition, more precisely, a phenomenon which is widespread owing to some intrinsic or at least non-specified condition, the popularized, presupposes a specific process inside which one could discern a certain degree of autonomy. On the other hand, the term popular signifies a widespread condition or state of affairs, which, even while exhibiting a certain degree of change or growth, has its main characteristic features. More precisely, it may be said that while the term "popular" normally connotes a type of culture of more or less static character, the term "popularized" connotes the very opposite, namely, a type of culture which is both widespread and wide-spreading as a result of organized social action.

In understanding the popular practices observed in Hindu child-rearing, child psychology, development of the child, the interaction between the mother and child, and the relations of the child with the family members who are generally referred to as caretakers, the literature either in written form or the oral traditions that are carefully recorded as folklore literature is highly useful. Like the divine mothers whose images are shown sometimes with the child on their laps or the child clinging close to their breasts, the human mothers also display their actions suggesting the ultimate oneness of seemingly independent beings in the Hindu Universe. In this context, it may be mentioned that we must learn to understand the psychology of the children who live amidst the complex but unified array of caretakers in the Hindu joint family.

It is observed that the human infant at birth has an apparently small number of needs that are described variously as the need for nourishment, warmth, the need to escape various stimulation and perhaps the need for affection from its mother. The physical needs include food, oxygen, temperature regulation, elimination of waste matter, sleep and protection from harmful environmental elements.[5]

From the folk tales and songs it is seen that the Hindu child is locked in its mother's embrace and that the mother's indulgent presence surrounds the child until around the age of five, while the father's discipline intervenes traumatically. The mother takes care of all the physical needs and attends the child from time to time to keep the surroundings of the child clean and tidy. By singing the lullubies the child will be treated with care and affection and makes it sleep without any disturbance or fear. When the child cries, its needs will be met with and be assured of its safety by attending to the physical needs by the mother accompanied by songs. The popular folk songs sung by the mothers in this connection are recorded in the studies conducted in folklore literature.[6]

For the development of the personality of the child the family is an essential requisite. It is the first social institution that concerns the child. In the family the child wants to gain recognition for its existence and individuality. In the Hindu family parents, children and pet animals forms a unit with definite positions and functioning meant for them. The members of the family as their property will inherit all these things and besides that it aspires for the acceptance from the society as it grows to meet its sociological needs. For the child to be recognized as an individual in the society it should be able to perform certain basic physical needs on its own such as speech, walking, expression of feelings, etc. For this the elders in the family train the children with patience, love and affection. The mother is the first person in the family to train the child to walk, talk and express its feelings in an acceptable way. The mother treats her child as the most beautiful one and that the beauty of nature is embodied in the child. Whatever little effort is made by the child in learning to talk and walk will be praised and appreciated by the mother, as it is known through the following popular songs.[7]

పాపాయి కన్నులూ కలువ రేకుల్లు
పాపాయి జులపాలు పట్టు కుచ్చుల్లు
పాపాయి దంతాలు మంచి ముత్యాలు
పాపాయి చేతుల్లు పొట్ల కాయల్లు
పాపాయి పలుకులు తేనెచిలుకుల్లు
పాపాయి చిన్నెల్లు బాలకృష్ణ వన్నెల్లు

Another song describes the beauty of a girl child:

చిక్కుడు పువ్వెరుపు చిలుక ముక్కెరుపు
చిగురెరుపు చింతల్ల దొండపండెరుపు
రక్కెస పండెరుపు రాగిచెంబెరుపు
ఆ ఎరుపు అమ్మాయి తన వారిలోన
- - - - - ... - -

Educating the child to eat the sweet rice-and-milk porridge is known by the following song:

లాలు పాసం లాలు
లాంగల్లి రెప్పల లాలు
ముద్దు మాణిక్యము లాలు
మురహరి తొక్కుపప్పు లాలు
లాలు లేవి నీ చెయ్యి నీటు
జూరుకో పాయసం జూరుకో!

Likewise the children were made to salute to the lamp and God from their early childhood.

రక్ష, రక్ష, సంధ్య రక్ష, సర్వ రక్ష, జీవ రక్ష,
దివ్య రక్ష చిన్ని నా అబ్బాయికి శ్రీరామ రక్ష.

The physical closeness between the mother and child is very much evident from folklore literature. The approach of the Hindu mother to the child is found to be a mixture of care and restrained acts to push the child outward, away from her and toward the group, consisting of the other members of the family, even as it reassures the child of her caring presence. In almost all the folk tales and the songs sung by the mothers to make the children to sleep, the physical closeness between the mother and the child is emphasized. For the first two years both of them are seldom apart due to the physical needs of the child. In the small world of the child, the mother plays a major role in attending to the needs of the child. Until the age of five, the average Hindu child does not enter the world of men and if no younger siblings arrive, he may at times periodically take the breast up to or even beyond the age. Around five years the child will be thrust into the orbit of its father and suddenly expected to grow up. He must help at home and obey the rules of caste and kinship. Now he must abandon the mother's embrace. Worse, his father remains a cool and distant authority figure. At times, it is observed that the Hindu childcare lacks in the gradual training in frustration tolerance, which is contrary to the child rearing practices followed in the West. The studies conducted earlier by psychoanalysts have revealed that the serenity and calm of a well-adjusted Hindu family life is a precarious calm based on suppressing rather than on resolving underlying tensions. The typical Hindu child rearing practices are essentially based on prolonged physical contact of the mother with the child involving breast feeding on demand and the traumatic shift of the child to the demanding orbit of the father at the age of five. Further, it is observed that the prolonged closeness of the Hindu child to the mother leaves it unprepared for independent activity and fearful of isolation. It may be mentioned here that the dominant Hindu cultural values and closely-knit family system are entirely consonant with the actions of the Hindu parents who do not prepare their child for independence. Possibly, this could be the main reason why the Hindus vlaue group solidarity over individual independence. Quite often it is reflected in the folk tales.[8]

In the society the status of the young mother is linked to the bearing of the male child. This is because of the importance attached to the masculine gender in the patriarchal society. The importance attributed to the male child to the mother prompts in her an untoward emotional investment which is unconsciously communicated to the child through excessive physical attention. The following songs reveal how the mother values and rejoices over the birth of the male child:

"మొగవాడు పుట్టాడు, మొగ్గ పుట్టాడు
ధనము పెట్టెలకెల్ల దాత కలిగాడు"

"స్వాతి వానలు కురిసె సంద్రాల కడను
పాల వానలు కురిసె బంధువుల యిండ్ల"

"కంటేను కొడుకుల్లు కాన్పే కనాలి
పిడికెడు విత్తనాలు మడికెల్ల చాలు
ఒక్కడే కొడుకైన వంశాన చాలు"

In turn some popular songs record the love and affection the child has towards its parents and parental home.

"పుట్టిన్నాటి నండి పువ్వోలె సాది — పున్నదా నేనెల్లు పుట్టిల్లు మరుతు
కన్న నాటి నుండి గార్వంగ సాది — కాముడా నేనెల్లు కన్న వార్ని మరుతు"
ఏరుపారిన పాటు ఏటిమీది యుటుక — తలుచుకున్న పాటు తల్లి మీద మర్లు.

It has been observed by Sudhir Kakar that the mother tends to perceive a son as a kind of saviour and to nurture him with gratitude and even reverence as well as with affection and care. For a range of reasons, the balance of nurturing is so affective that the mother unconsciously demands that the child serve as an object of her own unfulfilled desires and wishes however antithetical they may be to his own.[9] The child feels compelled to act as her saviour. Faced with her unconscious intimations and demands, it may feel confused, helpless and inadequate, frightened by its mother's nearness and yet unable to get away. Stanely N. Kurtz has critically examined this kind of analysis of the "seductive bad mother" theme in India proposed by Sudhir Kakar. He sates that the views of Kakar imply a Western style "intimacy" or "love relationship" between the mother and the child in the Indian context which in reality does not exist.[10] It is expressed that the emotional tone of the Hindu mother-child relationship is quite different from that found in the West and that the difference is best conceived of as one of kind rather than degree.

Various issues related to the Hindu child rearing practices are revealed through literature generated by ethnographic studies. Researchers have examined the emotional character of the Hindu mother-child relationship. Their observations reveal that the care of the children by the Hindu mother was casual and impersonal.[11] Children were taken for granted and their basic needs attended to but they received little other special attention or stimulation. It is mentioned that while children were greatly desired, once born, they were treated as one more member of the household, not as a special individual deserving of special attention. This has been explained as due to the taboos that prevailed against the over-praise or focusing of undue attention on infants for fear of attracting the evil eye or other mishappenings.

Thus the study of the child-rearing practices reveal the observational data on the physical contact of the mother with the child in its infancy to meet its physical needs sometimes as evidence of sensual over-indulgence and of extreme emotional closeness. It also throws light on how high the mother of a male child was valued in the society and how she rejoices over the birth of the male child through the popular folk traditions. It also explains the reasons for receiving little attention by the child from the mother due to some social taboos or superstitions. Further the oral and folk traditions that are prevalent till date examined here suggest the various Hindu child-rearing practices observed by the mother. It also projects the help offered by the mother to the child in its development not only physically, but also in acquiring all its skills and mental abilities.

References

1. E.J. Hobsbawn, "History from Below-Some Reflections" in Frederich Karntz ed., *History from Below: Studies in Popular Protest and Popular Ideology,* Oxford, 1988.
2. Isaac Sequera, *Popular Culture—East and West,* Delhi, 1991, p.47.
3. Peter Burke., *Popular Culture in Early Modern Europe,* London 1978; Barry Reay., ed. *Popular Culture in Early Modern England,* London, 1985: Zev Barby, "Popular Culture: A Sociological Approach" in C W E Bigsby., ed. *Approaches to Popular Culture,* London, 1976: Morag Shaich, *Discourse on Popular Culture: Class, Gender and History in Cultural Analysis 1730 to the Present,* London, 1989, p. 35; Stuart Clark, "French Historians and Early Modern Popular Culture" in *Past & Present,* No. 100, Aug. 1983, pp. 62-99.
4. Dai Smith., "What is History of Popular Culture?" in *What is History Today?* Ed. By Juliet Gardiner, London 1988.
5. George G. Thompson., *Child Psychology,* 2nd ed. 1965, p. 14.
6. P. Saraswati., *Janapada Sahityamu-Pillalapatalu,* Hyderabad, 1989; S. Lakshmi Narasamma., *Strila patalu-Oka Parisilana* Kakinada, 1989; Krishna Sri., "Lalipatalu-Melukolpulu", in Bharati, 1954.

7. N. Gangadharam., *Minneru,* Rajahmundry, 1968.
8. P. Saraswati., *op.cit.,* p. 101-103.
9. Sudhir Kakar., *Inner World A Psycho-Analytic Study of Childhood and Society in India,* New Delhi, 1978, pp. 88-89.
10. Stanely N Kurtz., "Psychoanalytic Approaches to Hindu Child Rearing: A Critique" in *Vishnu on Freud's Desk,* ed. By T.G. Vaidyanathan & Jeffrey J. Kripal Delhi, 1999, pp. 185-215.
11. *Ibid.,* p. 204.

2

Beliefs, Attitudes and Values in Medieval Andhra: Gleanings Through Epigraphs

The religious beliefs of the people of Andhra generally revolve around attaining salvation (*moksha*) and spiritual merit in the next world. To achieve these objectives people used to donate liberally to the temples or Brahmins. By choosing certain auspicious occasions and festivals they made donations and these were carefully inscribed on the walls and pillars of the temples. Although people used to take the sacred bath in the tanks situated in the temple precincts or in the waters of the rivers to which they attribute spiritual values before they worship the Gods, they rarely used to refer to them and its merits in their inscriptions. Likewise, the offering of blood or reference to the food mixed with blood in the stone inscriptions that are generally associated with some temples, is the unusual practice that one encounters in the study of the epigraphs of Andhra region. To understand the full significance of the contents of such rare inscriptions in the Andhra region an attempt is made here to analyse them critically and to focus on the hidden motives. As every action will have a hidden motive behind it and since the action is simply the behaviour of the persons with certain motives hidden or otherwise, must be examined in to give meaning to all such unusual actions. It intends to assess the beliefs and practices, the product of a specific historical and cultural situation rather than one with a timeless and universal quality, as every culture can only be judged by its own value system.

It is generally argued that beliefs, attitudes and values are all organized together to form a functionally integrated congnitive system, so that a change in any part of the system will affect the other parts, and will culminate in the behavioural change of the individuals. The countless beliefs that a person possesses would be retained in an unorganized chaotic state within the mind. However, these beliefs would somehow be organised into certain systems having describable and measurable structural properties, which would in turn become observable behavioural consequences[1]. Some of these beliefs are acquired or derived from some credible sources and therefore they play a greater influence on the behaviour of the individuals. Throughout the history man has been inspired by the religious motives and beliefs and has indeed espoused noble and humanitarian ideals and often behaved accordingly. A belief system represents within it, in some organized psychological but not necessarily logical form, each and every one of a person's countless beliefs about physical and social reality. The religious and superstitious beliefs recorded in the stone inscriptions will be examined here to know how they are developed? What motivational functions do such belief systems serve? What is the relation between the religious beliefs and human sufferings and what conditions facilitate that belief system to be recorded in the stone inscriptions at temples and so on? To find out the answers for these questions and other related issues two stone inscriptions are taken up for a detailed study.

An inscription from Vellaturu in Nalgonda district dated A.D. 1468 records the installation of the golden images of gods Virupaksha *linga*, Bhairava, Gaṇapati and Nāga by Śrī

Nityānanda *Maha Yogi* under the instructions of Śrī Mallikarjuna Mahalingam at Vellaturu and to the south of Pāpavināśēśvaradēva in the waters of the river Krishna[2]. It then refers to the merits of having a bath (*snāna*) in the waters and offering prayers to God. Here it is interesting to note that while referring to the merits of worshipping the gods, it mentions certain physical and mental ailments that could be cured and treated with success in eliminating them. If persons possessed by the demonic spirits bathe in the waters and offer salutations to the Gods, they will be liberated from the clutches of the spirits (*bhūtam*). In our country two kinds of mental illness are identified which include endogenous madness occurring because of excessive worrying, anxiety or some physical illness and spirit possession (*bhūta and prēta*). The cases of mental illness and psychic distress of the above two types were generally treated with some success by diviners, sorcerers, herbalists, palmists and horoscope specialists since the healing traditions and the therapeutic efforts practised by them combine elements from classical Indian astrology, medicine, magic with beliefs and practices from folk and popular traditions[3]. The restoration of mental and spiritual well being i.e, soul health is also sometimes attributed to the mystical-spiritual traditions.

The inscription under study then refers to the importance of bathing in the waters and offering salutations to the God incurring the physical ailments of the people including the curing of the people who were inflicted with snake bite. It adds that the poison that entered into the bodies will be made powerless with the grace of the God. If a person offers incense, lamp and *naivedya* for seven Mondays continuously without any break in between and if the husband and wife takes bath together in the waters of the river Krishna, it will result in getting progeny for the couple who are not blessed with children so far and for those, whose children die immediately after their birth would survive. Further it will help these people to become hale and healthy who suffer from intermittent fever that appears on every fourth day (*chatuttikam*). If a person takes a bath in the waters of the river in the above said manner, God will bless him and with his grace the dreadful disease like leprosy will be cured.

The ritual bathing and offering of prayers and salutations to the gods by worshipping them with lamp, incense and *naivedya* mentioned in the record are common to both men and women. The observance of the religious practices mentioned in the record would benefit the people who observe them and as a result the person who suffers from either mental or physical ill-health will be cured of his problems and the childless would beget children. From this it appears that concrete efforts have been made by the saints of the medieval times to encourage the people to follow the religious observances for their own merit. In order to keep alive certain religious traditions connected with the worshipping of the gods, the saints used to construe certain myths and beliefs to inspire the laymen to indulge themselves more and more in religious ritual practices. To sustain the vitality of the religious traditions and revivify the essential elements of religious myths that were propagated, the great saint (*Mahāyōgi*) Śrī Nityānanda has issued the inscription to popularize the religious concepts further by stating that the record was issued with the permission of (*ānatini*) Śrī Mallikārjuna Mahāliṅgam who is none other than the lord Mallikārjuna, for whom a great temple was constructed at Śrīśailam. Since the Śiva temple at Śrīśailam was very famous during the medieval times and had a large number of devotees, specific reference has been made in the present record to lord Mallikārjuna, probably with the idea to give wide publicity to the religious message contained in the record. The religious ritual practices conveyed through this record are quite simple and are found to be very easy to observe by childless couples, the mentally and physically sick people. But the main point stressed here is on bathing in the waters of the river Krishna and venerating the gods installed at the temple. These religious beliefs propagated through the stone inscriptions help in promoting the pilgrimage network that connects the important Śaiva temples in the Andhra region. It appears that the intention of publicizing the merits and the benefits of worshipping the gods was to attract the pilgrims in large numbers so that the status of the temple could be elevated from its local level to the regional level and that it would gain material benefits through the many endowments made by the devotees. Further the conduct of the rituals mentioned in the inscription also has got some social significance as its observance would ensure good health, longevity and progeny to the observers besides the grace of the gods. Perhaps it is with the intention to establish a continuous religious belief and tradition that the popular myths were constructed laying great emphasis on the well-being of the devotees in this world, which are not usually met with in the contemporary inscriptions of the Andhra region. The performance of the rituals and practices are essentially social in nature as it involves the participation of the members of the family. It symbolizes the feeling of a whole community, which promotes close relations creating solidarity and group or cultural identity among the devotees.

As a result of the fusion of the brahmanical and (village) folk religions certain Hindu temples have conducted some tantric religious practices that involve the offering of blood or food cooked with blood[4]. The tantric ritual practices possess a healing system for the physical and mental illness of the human and animal beings and contains a modest theory of the causes and relief of certain forms of mental distress[5]. An undated inscription from Rapur in Nellore district refers to some tantric ritual practices followed by the people mentioning some *mantras* including some mystical syllables and offering of food cooked with blood[6]. Reference has been made to the village gods and goddesses that reside at the boundaries of the villages namely, Bhūdēvī, Anjanīdēvī, Pittalamma, Varavari and the god Paśunātha, the lord of animals in the inscriptions along with the mention of some tantric *mantras* like *Ōṁ, Hraṁ, Śrīṁ, Hrīṁ, Vaṭṭu, Bhaṭṭu, Svāhā, Bēla paṭṭu, Phatu* and *Svāhā* in that order. It then states that a pit should be dug at the entrance of the cattle-shed to cook food, draw milk from the cow, then offer incense, lamp and put three marks of blood on the face (*mūṇḍu netturu boṭlu peṭṭi*) and distribute the food cooked with blood (*eṛṛakūḍu*) to the people present there. Further it provides details with regard to the preparation of the medicine to be administered to the sick animals through a tube. In this context it mentions the items like *mārēḍu* (*aegle marmelos*), *donḍakūra* (*coccinea indica*), gingelly, *buduṃa* (*cucunis*), mustard, salt, pepper, garlic, urine (kalumadi), jaggery and sour butter milk. It is mentioned at the end of the record that one has to pay obeisance to the god (mrokkuulu veṭṭedi). It may be mentioned here that the nature of the disease for which this kind of medicine was prescribed was not referred to. From this record it is observed that by uttering certain *mantras* mentioned in the record and by offering to the gods as *naivedya* the food cooked with blood, the devotees were intended to seek the blessings of the village deities. Generally, the main objective in venerating the village deities is found to be to please them with blood sacrifices and offerings to avert their wrath on the villagers and their cattle wealth. Sometimes it is also to get rid of the contagious and epidemic diseases that spread widely in the villages. Another popular belief that spread among the villagers was the possession of the persons and animals by the spirits (*bhūta* and *prēta*). Probably for any such reasons or specifically to ward off the evil spirits from the village boundaries, the stones inscribed with some magic formulae along with the names of the village deities were installed at the village Rapur[7]. Further it also gives support to the people's perception of the medieval times that diseases would be caused by the gods when they were not pleased with the people and when they were not well propitiated by their offerings. The specific reference to the kind of the preparation of the medicine with herbs, jaggery, urine, etc., for the sick animals suggests the medicinal knowledge of the people of the medieval times and also their intention to publicise both the medicinal formula to cure sick animals and the magical words (*mantras*) used to obtain the grace of the village deities for the well-being and benefit of the people of future generations.

Thus the study of the two stone records reveals the popular beliefs of the people associated with the religious faiths i.e. Śaivism and worshipping of village deities for the achievement of good health, general well-being and progeny for the people and curing the diseases of the animals. It thus throws a welcome light on the hidden intentions of the great saint to publicise the greatness as well as the importance of the sacred bath and worshipping of the golden images of the gods installed by him through the stone record for the continuity of the religious practices to be observed in the temple at Vellaturu. A study of the popular beliefs and religious ritual practices thus acts as a mirror which reflects the images of religion, material culture, human behaviour, human attitudes, hidden intentions, motivations and value system of the medieval Andhra that would otherwise be known imperfectly to the academic world.

References

1. Milton Rokeach, *Beliefs, Attitudes and Values : A Theory of Organization and Change,* London, 1968.
2. P.V. Parabrahma Sastry, *Inscriptions of Andhra Pradesh, Nalgonda District,* vol. I, Hyderabad, 1992, no. 150 (A.R. No. 19 of 1973).
3. Sudhir Kakar, *Shamans in India and its Healing Traditions,* Delhi, 1982, p. 4.
4. M. Krishna Kumari, *Studies on Medieval Andhra History and Culture,* Delhi, p. 118; Also see R.N. Nandi, *Religious Institutions and Cults in the Deccan A.D. 600-1000,* Delhi, 1973, p. 115.
5. Sudhir Kakar, *op.cit.,* p. 152.
6. *Inscriptions of Nellore District* Part III, Rapur 16, p. 1225-1227.
7. S.S. Ramachandra Murthy, "Andhra Epigraphs and Folklore" in *Journal of the Epigraphical Society of India,* vol. XII, 1985 pp. 77-88.

3

Riddles and Proverbs as Sources of the Social History of Andhradesa

Riddles, proverbs, charms, nursery rhymes and tongue twisters are all the examples of fixed phrase folklore forms. There may be over all variation with respect to a given riddle or proverb as it is told by different members of the same culture, but one individual person will always recite the riddle or proverb using exactly the same words. Here an attempt has been made not to demonstrate the literary art or merit in the language used in the proverbs and riddles but to comprehend and appreciate the social context, subtleties and beauty of the composition as well as to highlight their importance as a source for understanding the family relations among the members of the family and the social values that prevailed in the then society.

Riddles are part of the culture of a people and are educational since they are varied in content, but their primary aim is to provide entertainment and recreation. They refer to the nature as a whole, and to the material and spiritual culture, of the people. Because of the amusement that the riddles provide the young people favour them while the old people encourage their use due to their instructive value. Riddles are socially and culturally significant and it is very much evident from the form and content of the riddles. Like the other folklore materials such as customs, beliefs, folk tales and folk songs, the riddles and proverbs are the product of dynamic mental processes, the response of the folk soul to either the outer or inner needs, the expression of various longings, fears, aversions or desires. In Andhra, the riddles are popularly known as *poḍupu kathalu*. However, a few other terms are also in usage in different parts of Andhra. They are *taṭṭu, artham, aḍḍu katha, oḍḍu katha, cikku muḷḷu, ciṭkālu, ciṭukulu, māru kathalu, mārutaṭṭu, yaksha praśnalu, vippē kathalu, smasyalu or samiccalu* and *śāstram.*[1] The riddles are played by the people-both young and old, when they found leisure time or during the festival days.

From the study of the riddles collected from the Andhra region by the folklorists it appears that for the majority of riddles the answer consists of one word only. Sometimes either two words or one sentence would be the answer. It is also observed that, among the players of the riddles, the explanation is often given in obscure terms and, therefore, the answers to such obscure riddles are learnt by heart by the people. Riddles deal mainly with the material world surrounding the people. In the riddles is described nature as a whole, particularly numerous being the riddles, which refer to the natural phenomena, the flora and fauna, from insects and grass to trees and elephants. They also commonly describe material objects in the culture of the people. Most of the riddles are related to the things used in the common village household like pots, lamps, fire, smoke, matchsticks, churners, leaves, vegetable cutter, crescent shaped sword, hand stick, cow dung, battle-axe, broomstick, ladder, cot, lock, keys, etc. Next in importance occupy the riddles referring to the food items, vegetables, corn, coconut, etc. The knowledge of human physiology is well composed in the riddles. They refer to the eyes, eye-lids, eye-balls, teeth, nose, beard, fingers, hair, moustache, lips, etc. Some riddles refer to the sky, stars, moon, Sun, rainfall, thunder, clouds, year, months, days, moon light and rainbow. The knowledge of the different types of animals, birds and varieties of fruits can also be gathered from the study of the riddles of Andhra.

To understand the marriage customs and practices the historians have to depend largely on the literary sources. Even then, sometimes they do not provide either detailed description or information about certain social practices, which were in vogue during the past and are continued till today. In this context, reference may be made to the *ayirēṇi* pots. These are the pots specially made and decorated with colourful designs by the potters for the purpose of marriage ceremonies. Before the marriage both the bride and bridegroom were made to sit before the *ayireni* pots and worship them. These pots are treated as the symbols of goddess Lakshmī and worshipped by men and women alike.[2] In the literary work *Vijaya Vilāsamu* it is mentioned that the women of the marriage party go to the potter's house with music and lamps and bring the *ayireni* pots carefully with lamps and singing songs to the place where the marriage is going to be celebrated (*ayirēṇi goni vaçç raiduval paṭalu pāḍucu subha vēḍukalara*). The social and religious importance of the *ayirēṇi* pots in the social life of the people is thus referred to in the literature of the medieval period. On the other hand, the inscriptions of 12th century A.D. refer to *ayirēṇi rūka* in the context of the taxes collected by the State. Although no further details are provided in the inscriptions with regard to the actual meaning and significance of the term *ayirēṇi ruka,* it can be comprehended from the references contained in *Vijaya Vilāsamu* that it relates to the marriage ceremonies. On the other hand, the riddles as well as the folk songs that are popular among the Andhras and collected carefully by the folklorists, reveal the true purpose and nature of *ayirēṇi* in explicit terms. The riddles like *paccala paṁdiṭlo maccala guṟṟam* (the spotted horse in the colourful pandal), *pacca miṭhāyi, tiṁṭe nōraṁtā pāḍeye* (the colourful sweet that spoils the mouth when it is eaten) reveal that the *ayirēṇi* pots are painted in colours and designs which make them very attractive in appearance.[3] Further the presence of the *ayirēṇi* pots is essentially associated with the marriage pandal. In conducting the marriage ceremony special significance is attached to the tying up of *tāḷi* by the bridegroom on the neck of the bride and it forms the essential part of the marriage. The importance of the *tāḷi* is well reflected in the following riddles and the answer for these riddles is *tāḷi* or *tāḷboṭṭu*.[4]

* "*Ākāku, ariṭāku, adilēṁde pani jaragadu*" (It is a leaf, plantain leaf, without which the purpose will not be served)
* "*iṁtiṁtāku, brahmaṁtāku, peddalu teccina pēruṁṭāku*" (the leaf as big as that of Brahma's leaf and the leaf brought by the elders)
* "*Guṇṭūru guṭṭa, Ēlūru miṭṭa, padimaṁdi paṭṭa, okkaḍe kaṭṭa*" (It is like the small hill of Guntur and Eluru; It will be touched by ten people but only one person can tie it)
* "*Tūnikalo beṭṭi tūcharu, aṁgaṭlo beṭṭi ammaru*" (It will not be weighed, it will not be sold in the market)

From the above riddles it can be gathered that the elders will bring the *tali* and will be touched by at least ten while one person can tie it up. While referring to it the shape of the *tāḷi* is suggested as that of a leaf and elevated in the centre. Another regular and essential practice in marriage is stamping on the feet of the bride by the bridegroom and walking together for seven steps. This age old practice has not been referred to in the other historical sources and it can be successfully gathered from the riddles and sayings. For example, the riddle "*Kaṁchilo okkālu, Kāmākshilo okkālu, nī aḍugulō nā aḍugu*" (One foot at Kaṁchi, one foot at Kāmākshī; my footstep in your footstep) suggests the practice of taking seven steps together by the married couple.[5]

Another important customary practice observed by the householders in Andhra from the ancient times that has parallels in the neighbouring regions also is the decoration of floors in front of the houses and temples by laying designs with white powder and colours generally referred to as *mṛuggulu peṭṭuṭa*. Rarely we get references to such practice from the inscriptions and literature of the medieval periods. Particularly the stone inscriptions from Simhachalam temple mention the practice as well as the people engaged for the purpose of decoration of the floors in the temples.[6] The types of designs and their names can be gathered from the Telugu literary works like *Nītisīsapadya Śatakamu* of Tallapaka Tirumalarya, *Haṁsaviṁśati* of Ayyalaraju Narayanamatya and *Śukasaptati* of Palavekari Kadiripati. These decorations on the floors form the content of the riddles in Andhra of which some are given below:[7]

* "*Tellagā vuṁṭuṁdi, gaḍapalō vuṁṭuṁdi cūcēvāḷḷanu pilustuṁdi*" (It is white in colour, it lies in front of the entrance, it calls upon the onlookers)
* "*Padahāru kommala vaṭavṛiksham paḍite lēvalēdu*" (It is a tree with sixteen branches; It cannot rise up when once it falls down)
* "*Mā iṁṭi muṁdara taṭṭa vēste ettēki rādu*" (When the basket is laid in front of our house, it cannot be lifted)
* "*Mā iṁṭlo paṭṭumaṁchaṁ, eṁta lēpinā lēvadu*" (The cot in my house will not rise howsoever much one tries)
* "*Midde mīdi kōlāṭam, vēsēvāre gāni tīsēvāru lēru*" (It is the folk dance *kōlāṭam* on the elevated place; one can put it but no one can remove it)
* "*Veṁḍi golusulu veyyaḍamē gāni tiyyaḍamē lēdu*" (The silver chains that can be placed and cannot be removed)
* *Venneṭlo Veṁḍi tīgelu* (The silver strings in the moon light)

From these riddles it can be understood that the *mṛuggus* are commonly laid with white flour in front of the houses, and when once it is drawn it cannot easily be removed. Further it also points out the nature and dimension of the *mṛuggus* as having been spread like a tree that spreads with its sixteen branches. This kind of information from the riddles is highly useful in the better understanding of the social customs and practices as it supports the stray references contained in the historical sources.

Besides the riddles the Andhras possess a rich folklore tradition comprising most importantly tales, songs, proverbs and sayings. Proverbs are by far the most frequently employed of these forms of verbal art and are used in all manner of situations—as a means of amusement, in educating the young, to sanction institutionalized behaviour as a method of gaining favour in court, in performing religious rituals and ceremonies and to give points and add colour to ordinary conversation.[8] A good number of proverbs recollected by the people of Andhra region are carefully collected and published by folklorists. The social and cultural context of the proverbs and the meaning that they convey provide a good source of information on the social history of Andhra. Like the riddles, proverbs are educational in their content, which is based on experience. The educational value of the riddles is a consequence of their cultural content, but their primary purpose is entertainment. It is observed that the proverb is a part of everyday speech while the riddles are often the concern of only one section of the community, and the playing of the riddles depends largely on the leisure time available. It follows then that the riddles have a more restricted function than the proverbs, in spite of the fact that they are an integral part of the people's culture and traditions like the proverbs.

The role of the mother-in-law in the family and her social relations with her daughter-in-law and the role of the son-in-law and his family relations can be known from several proverbs that are in usage in Andhra.[9] The content of the proverbs will also gain support by the other folklore materials like the folk tales and folk songs. The proverbs given below reveal the popular views of the people towards the mother-in-law in the family system.[10]

* "*Atta kālamukonnāḷḷu-kōḍali kālamukonnāḷḷu*" (The mother-in-law will have her time for some days; the daughter-in-law will have her time for some days)

* "*Atta chēsina paniki āraḷḷu lēvu*" (No criticism for the work done by the mother-in-law)

* "*Attaku maṁchi lēdu, Chiṁtaku pacci lēdu*" (There is no good thing about the mother-in-law, there is no tamarind that is not ripe)

* "*Atta sommu alluḍu dānamu cesinaṭlu*" (It is like the son-in-law who has donated money to the mother-in-law)

* "*Attavāriṁṭi sukhaṁ mōcēṭi debba*" (The comforts felt in the house of the mother-in-law will be like those of the strokes at the back of the fore-arm)

* "*Ḍabbunna vāriṁṭlo cinna kōḍalavaḍam kaṁṭe pēdiṁṭ lo pedda kōḍalavaḍamē mēlu*" (It is better to be the first daughter-in-law in a poor family than the youngest daughter-in-law in a rich family)

* "*Kōdalu iṁṭlo aḍugeḍte attaku Gaṁge dikku*" (When the daughter-in-law enters the house, the river Ganges is the only resort for the mother-in-law)

* "*Atta caccina arnellaku kōḍalu ēḍcinaṭlu*" (The daughter-in-law bemoans the death of her mother-in-law full six months after her death)

The above proverbs demonstrate well the nature of the family relations, the role of the mother-in-law in the family and the perceptions of the daughter-in-law towards her. The proverb being a part of everyday speech occasionally expresses some profound human truths. It is difficult to gather from the historical sources the kind of human and family relations, the sentiments and beliefs as they are reflected in the proverbs. The proverbs and riddles are a good reflection of the reactions of the people to people, things, or their interest therein. A careful collection and documentation of the riddles and proverbs besides the other folklore materials and the judicious usage and analysis will help the historians in understanding the social and cultural history in a comprehensive way. Further the great variety of contents and forms and their social importance make the riddles and proverbs of Andhra region a most interesting and inspiring subject of study for the folklorists as well as for the historians.

References

1. G.N. Reddi., *Poḍupu Kathalu* (Telugu) Tirupati, 1988 p.i.
2. Y. Raghuma Reddi., *Palle Padālalo Prajā Jīvanamu,* Jadcherla, 1979, pp. 276-277.
   B. Ramaraju., *Folklore of Andhra Pradesh,* Delhi, 1978.
3. G.N. Reddi., *op.cit.*, p. 119, no. 9; p. 112, no. 1.
4. *Ibid.*, p. 14, no. 8; p. 24, no. 5; p. 58, no. 4; p. 86, o. 4.
5. *Ibid.*, p. 44, no. 4.
6. M. Krishna Kumari., *Facets of Andhra Culture,* Delhi, 1999, pp.155-161.
7. G.N. Reddi., *op.cit.*, p. 50, no. 9; p. 87, no. 3; p. 113, no. 9; p. 134, no. 9; p. 135, no. 8; p. 136, no. 5; p. 153, no. 4; p. 153, no. 8.
8. Alan Dundes., The Study of Folklore, New Jersy, 1965, pp.187.
9. R.V.S. Sundaram., *Āndhrula Jānapada Vijñānamu,* Hyderabad, 2nd edition, 192 pp. 1885.
10. *Ibid.*, p. 191.

4

Psychohistorical Analysis of Curses and Folklore Traditions of Medieval Andhradesa

The seamy side of the social life of the people of medieval Andhra has not drawn the adequate attention it deserves from the historians due to the lack of specific historical sources on these aspects of study. However, the emotional history of the people could be projected with new tools of research such as psychoanalysis. Psychoanalysis is a historical science that illuminates the present precisely by concerning itself with the past. Psychoanalytic insights into the religious traditions which are sometimes mystical would give meaningful interpretations with regard to the psychological complexities that are responsible for certain ideas and practices followed by the people. Psychoanalysis as a tool of historical research, though not an absolute truth, has the potential to push the thinker into new, sometimes terrifying, frontiers of experience and consciousness. But its greatest weakness lies in its zeal to explore new regions and new questions, and in that process the methcd inevitably makes mistakes, sometimes goes too far and wanders into the dead ends of its own reified categories. On the other hand, its merits lie in its passion for ignoring convention and speaking out shocking truths, which are often extreme. It generally operates out of the assumption that dreams, myths, rituals and visions contain meanings that are not readily available on the surface; consequently, it is a method that prevents us from simply asking members of the culture what they think the symbol or the traditional practice means. With its respectful exploratory probes psychonalysis tries to read mental phenomena as half appearance whose full meanings must be deciphered and read out of the unconscious and the body from which they always arise. It thus is an essentially subversive practice, for it sets for itself the task of denying the social censor that constructed the mind's language, values and categories.[1] In this way Psychoanalysis goes well beyond the anthropologists' field study and the phenomenological study of the historians' to answer questions that no interview, text or phenomenological study is willing to ask and answer.

In the present paper an attempt has been made to analyse certain curses which are repeatedly mentioned in the Telugu stone inscriptions of medieval Andhra and certain folklore traditions reflecting oedipal complexes of the characters of the stories in relation to the Hindu mythological legends contained in the Sanskrit and Telugu works and to show how the psychoanalytical attitude might help us to understand properly the inner psyche of the people in construing such stereotyped curses and to solve the traditionally puzzling features. In the inscriptions of the medieval period while mentioning the imprecatory verses, reference has been made quite often to the undesirable and abhorrent sexual relations of human beings with animals such as dogs, donkeys, horses and pigs. In that context, the inscriptions also state that the results of unholy sexual relations with members of the family such as incest with mother, sister would befall on the persons who violate the grants donated. The contents of the inscriptions have been analysed earlier from the social and art-historical perspective providing the apotropaic explanation for the erotic imagery including the scenes of bestiality on the temple walls of the medieval times.[2] But here it is aimed to understand the inner meanings, the psyche and the context under which certain social sins were repeatedly mentioned in the inscriptions in the form of curses. In the Hindu literary texts certain odd circumstances and unlawful family relations are generally explained as the result of someone's actions in the remote past. Further, such situations are either justified or interpreted in accordance with the *karma* philosophy as the result of the personal intervention in the form of a curse, of a specific individual whose anger has been aroused.[3] The imprecatory passages included at the end of the inscriptions are also in the form of curses to instil terror in the minds of the people who would violate the conditions of the grant given for safeguarding them. The curses mentioned in them were also referred to as *mahā pātakas* that would bring misery and destruction for those who obstruct the terms and conditions of the grants. From the point of view of psycho historical inquiry the curses are treated as the internal fears and psyche of the people in the medieval Andhra society. Such types of apprehensions of the people that are documented and repeatedly referred to in the inscriptional literature and also reflected in the erotic imagery are not simply baseless. It further leads to begin with a search for an element of reality that underlies the phenomenon in question. Studies conducted by Freud and his followers have shown that there is in a sense no such thing as a baseless fear or belief. Therefore it can be said that the works of art, the curses or dreams represent real feelings and experiences, but in disguised forms. Beliefs in certain things or cherishing certain beliefs by the people would seem to be not because that the people are either ignorant or unenlightened but because the belief in something unreal satisfies some real, compelling and shared need.

The carnal desires exhibited by the father towards his daughter and those of the daughter towards her father are well represented in the Hindu mythological stories. One such example is the story of Brahmā's incest with his daughter as narrated in *Śivapuraṇa.*[4] Very soon the daughter realizes her folly and then she immolates herself in fire with the view to purify herself. As a result she obtains the boon that she will be reborn as Arundhatī, the exemplary of chaste wife, that her husband will be merely a close friend to her and finally, that any man who looks upon her with desire will become impotent. It may be mentioned here that Arundhati was responsible to establish officially the moral law that creatures before adolescence will not be subject to desire. To expiate her sin she was reborn as a child and protected herself as a child from any possibility of the infant sexuality from which she has suffered in such a blatant way. Further, she protects herself by diffusing her political aggressors by turning them into children and by the measure of unmanning them.[5] The *Matsya Purāṇa* and *Śatapatha Brāhmaṇa* contained the ancient myths that bear witness to a father's desire for his daughter in which the Creator God, Brahmā cast his eyes upon Gāyatrī.[6] According to the positive Oedipus story that appeared in the *Matsya Purāṇa*, when Brahma was engaged in the task of Creation, goddess Gāyatrī appeared in the form of one half of Brahmā's body who mistakenly took her for his daughter. Seeing the beauty of the goddess Brahmā immediately fell in love with her for whom the sons of Brahmā have expressed contempt and indignation for his act, which ultimately resulted in the losing of all the powers that Brahmā had acquired by asceticism. The incestuous relations and the disturbance caused to the normal kin relations were all looked down upon and, particularly, the sons would seem to react immediately in such cases against such erring fathers.

To detect the unconscious incestuous fantasies in the minds of the people and to understand the closeness of the mother and son with the father left out, it is essential to mention here the Oedipus like patterns in the folklore traditions of Andhra and suggest an interpretation. According to the local traditions prevalent in Rajahmundry and elsewhere in Andhra the area known as Sārangadhara Meṭṭa is closely associated with the event of the blinding of the eyes of prince Saranga by the king. According to the folk tale Chitrāngī, the stepmother of prince Sāranga, desires her stepson, who rejects her advances. When he rejects her, she accuses him of making improper advances to her and as a result his father punishes him by blinding his eyes and mutilating his limbs. The rivalry between father and son for the mother is because the mother loves her son and the father is left out. In Oedipus complex, blinding is a well-recognized symbol for castration. The Oedipus situation in the female presents certain peculiarities. Particularly among the Indian women, the desire to have a male child in preference to a female is almost universal. Another popular folk tale in Andhra with regard to the rivalry of father to his son is mentioned in the Telugu literary work *Suka Saptati*. In this story a father returns home after a long period and got enraged to see a strange young man sleeping by the side of his wife when he saw them through a window. Instantaneously, he then draws his sword to kill him, but was stopped when his attention was drawn towards a verse containing the precept stating, "don't act when angry". In fact the young man is his son, grown to manhood during his long absence, but still sleeping along with his mother. From the few instances cited above, it is observed that the Indian Oedipus pattern is such that—like sexes repel, while unlike sexes attract. Studies revealed that while the Western son wishes to supplant the father, the tales cited from the Indian context show that the Indian father (story of Brahmā) wishes to marry his own daughter. Similarly, the mother desires her own son. The reverse, defensive and negative Oedipus type as reflected in the Hindu mythological tales is contrary to the positive Oedipus type of Western culture wherein the son marries his mother castrating or fighting with his father. The basic difference between these two types of Oedipus can be interpreted as due to the cultural, psychological and other factors including the child rearing practices, patterns of emotional development and the social institutions, etc. The subjective material from the local traditions and Hindu mythological stories considered and analysed here provides the inner meaning of the external behaviour expresed in the form of curses in the epigraphs with regard to the undesirable family relations that should be avoided. Although there is no one clear word for "incest" used in the Indian languages, there are a series of words used for the crime of sexual intercourse in the bed of the guru (*guru talpābhigamana*). This offence is included in their codes by Manu and by other *Dharmaśāstra* writers among the great sins (*mahā pātakas)* along with brahmicide. To this list of crimes are added in the Telugu inscriptional literature the sins of sexual intercourse with one's own mother and sister. It is observed from the *Dharmaśāstra* literature that to their definition of the incestuous sin of intercourse with a guru's wife, they add a list of other sins of the same form (*tadrūpya*) or equal (*sāmya)*.[7] Incestuous sexual relations are also prescribed in the *Tantra* which appears as a relic of a very old custom.[8] In the *Vājasanēyi Saṁhitā,* Ambikā was referred to as the sister of Rudra. The commentary of the *Suttanipāta* refers to the Śākyas who were rebuked by the Koliyars for cohabiting like dogs with their own sisters.[9] The incestuous affairs appear to have had some ritual significance. It is observed that the Ṛgvēda contained the incestuous dialogue of Yama and Yāmī in which the sister in passionate words, glowing with desire, draws the brother on to love.[10] These references and the custom of sister marriage referred to in the Jain work *Avasyaka Çūrṇi* reveal that the incestuous sexual relation was a social reality.

Another type of curse frequently mentioned in the medieval Telugu inscriptions is related to the sexual relations of human beings with different animals. An inscription from Ongole dated A.D. 1314 states that the persons who misappropriate the grant will be considered to have committed incest with his sister and to have allowed his wife to be covered by a donkey.[11] Several stone epigraphs of 15th and 16th centuries A.D. of Andhra region contain the imprecatory passages to the effect that if the endowments made were either misappropriated or not properly maintained, the offender's wife will be ravished by the animals like dogs, donkeys, elephants, horses and pigs.[12] It has been observed by the historians like D.C. Sircar, V. Upadhyay, R.N. Saletore and Bhagawanlal Indraji that in many parts of India are found *gārdabha* stones having the depiction of a donkey or some other animal with a woman along with the inscription of a curse from about 10th century A.D.[13]

In the temple art of medieval times, scenes of bestiality are observed in two types in which the figures include man copulating with an animal and the animal mating with the figures of woman.[14] Of these types, generally men of aristocratic appearance have relations with a horse, donkey, bear or dog; while the donkey, the beast of burden, has relations with a woman. On the *prākāra* wall of the temple at Srisailam of Kurnool district are found a few sculptures with bestiality as its main theme. It may be mentioned here that although the idea of mating between human beings and beasts had been denounced vehemently by Vātsyāyana in his *Kāmasūtra,* such scenes had gained popularity throughout India. Studies conducted earlier on this subject have shown that such type of erotic themes on the temple walls would serve the protective function for the temple structures besides being the decorative motifs.[15]

This notion of the bestiality seen in the art forms is vehemently condemned and looked down upon in the classical literature. However, while tracing the roots of such practices it is found that it has not gone totally unnoticed in the Hindu mythological legends. It is referred to in a story that the king got sexual desires towards the animal when he touches the genital organs of the animal through which he got a son. In the *Mārkaṇḍēya Purāṇa* translated into Telugu by Marana there is an interesting episode in which king Surashtra who was blessed with long life had lost all his hundred wives, close relatives and ministers. After entrusting the kingship to

Vimarda he went to the forest. One day when there was a heavy rain, the king lost his way in the total darkness and was washed away in the running waters of the river stream. At that time, he could catch hold of a deer by its tail in the running water and accidentally he touched the genital organs of the animal by which he got sexual desires on the animal, as he enjoyed the happiness through his touch. As a result he got a son by name Tāmasa and the king was told later that the animal by which he got a son was none other than his chief queen.[16] A different version of the birth of Gaṇēśa is mentioned in *Suprabhēdāgama* according to which when Śiva went to the forest on the slopes of the Himalayas in the company of Pārvatī to enjoy each other's company, the found a male and female elephants in the act of mating. On visualizing this Śiva and Pārvatī got sensuously excited and by assuming the elephant forms they enjoyed themselves sexually as a result of which was born Gaṇeśa with the face of an elephant.[17]

In Kauṭilya's *Arthaśāstra* it is stated that when a senseless man has sexual intercourse with beasts, he shall be fined 12 *panas* and when he commits the same act with idols of goddesses (*dēvatā pratimā*) he shall be fined twice as much.[18] Therefore, it is evident from this early work on state craft that the apprehension and fears of the people of the medieval times with regard to the acts of bestiality expressed in the form of curses are not completely unfounded and that they were treated as crimes and that the culprits were imposed with fines during the ancient times. Although outwardly the curses under study may appear as the irrational fears of the people, in reality they may either disguise or mask genuine events and real anxieties from such events as the underlying experiences are so menacing and traumatizing that the conscious mind of the people cannot cope with them effectively. On the other hand, it may reflect a real and widely shared human experience, which are subject to repression and relegated to the unconscious mind. But ultimately, they re-emerged as curses in the disguised and more tolerable form and were treated as the social sins of the medieval times. Although traditional Telugu literature does have very few references to the Oedipal desires, the popular folk traditions widespread in the Andhra region had represented them in fictitious form. Thus the study attempts to trace the roots of origin for Oedipal complex and also for the unnatural sexual desires through the literary and folklore traditions. It further helps in attempting a new interpretation to look for the real elements that were responsible for the formulation of curses in a stereotyped manner in the stone epigraphs of the medieval times.

References

1. Richard Shweder., *Thinking through Cultures: Explorations in Cultural Psychology,* Cambridge: Harvard University Press, 1991, p. 99.
2. M. Krishna Kumari., *Studies on Medieval Andhra History and Culture,* Delhi 1994, pp. 58-59.
3. Robert P Goldman., "Karma, Guilt and Buried Memories: Public Fanasy and Private Reality in Traditional India" in T.G. Vaidyanathan and Jeffrey J. Kripal., *Vishnu on Freud's Desk : A Reader in Psychoanalysis and Hinduism.,* Delhi 1999, pp. 250-278.
4. *Śivapurāṇa.,* 2.2.5-7.
5. Sudhir Kakar., *The Inner World: A Psycho Analytic Study oj Childhood and Society in India,* Delhi, 1978, p. 90.
6. T.G. Vaidyanathan and Jeffrey J. Kripal, *op.cit.,* p. 122.
7. *Ibid.,* p. 121.
8. N.N. Bhattacharya, *History of Tantric Religion,* Delhi 1999, p. 131.
9. *Kuṇāla Jātaka,* no. 536, p. 412.
10. *Ṛgveda,* X 10.
11. A. Butterworth., *A Collection of Inscriptions on the Copper Plates and Stones in the Nellore District,* Ongole, 7.
12. *S.I.I.* vol. XVI 331; A. Butterworth., *op.cit.,* Ongole 115; Nellore 33, 24; Kanigiri 5.
13. D.C. Sircar., *Indian Epigraphy,* p. 89.
14. M. Krishna Kumari., *op.cit.,* p. 58.
15. Thomas E. Donaldson., "Propitious-Apotropaic Eroticism in the Art of Orissa," *Artibus Asiae,* vol XXXVII, pp. 77ff; Urmila

Agrawal., "Mithunas: Why Obscene Sculptures?" *Orienal Art,* XIV, 1968, p. 260.

16. *Mārkandeya Purānamu* of Marana (ed) by G.V. Subahmanyam, A.P. Sahitya Academy, Hyderabad, 1984 Canto 5, v. 223-248, pp. 303-305.
17. T.A. Gopinatha Rao., *Elements of Hindu Iconography.*, vol. I, Part I Delhi 2nd ed., 1971, pp. 44-45.
18. *Arthaśāstra.*, op.cit., Book IV, ch. XII. 236, p. 268.

5

Psychoanalytical and Iconographical Perceptions of Mother and Child

For the individual and personality development the first months of human life, a period of worldless oblivion, is of great significance. For all later psychological experiences infancy and childhood are the foundations. The nature of an individual's first relationship with one's own mother influences profoundly the quality and "dynamics" of social relations throughout one's life. The ideals of motherhood, the parental care of the children and the crucial role of this relationship for the development of all subsequent social relations are well recognized and demonstrated in Indian art and literature. The psychological reciprocity between the mothers and infants were well elaborated by Sigmund Freud. While explaining the importance of the mothers to the infants, he described it as "unique, without parallel, established unalterably for a whole life-time as the first and strongest love object and as the prototype of all later love relations for both genders".[1] In spite of the significance of the mother-child relations, it remains to be intellectually elusive and relatively unexplored. However, the works of the psychologists, anthropologists and psycho historians in this direction are preoccupied with the feeding and nurturing of the infants to know about the emotional climate and the gestures of mothering and nurturing. In this context the appreciation of Hindu art forms would be of great usefulness as they help in the better undersanding of mother-infant relations in India as the central dynamic factor in the personality formation of the people in Indian culture. This is because a person first learns to relate to the "other" and begins to develop his capacity to love from the mother-infant relations. Further it is from these relations that an individual originates as a social being and, as an adult, all his affiliations and intimacies bear the stamp of one's own particular kind of infancy that was experienced. In this context, an attempt is made here to appreciate the iconography of the relief sculptures of mother and infant with special reference to a stone slab exhibited in the British Museum, London, to highlight the mother-infant relationship as reflected in art forms in ancient India. It also deals with the stone sculptures of *Saptamātrikas* and a few images of *Yōginīs* who were shown with a child on their laps to project the feelings of warmth, intimacy and affection between the mother and child.

Several stone sculptures of the mother and child are reported from Central, Northern and Eastern India and are found to be a favourite theme of the artists of Eastern India. The main theme of the sculpture is the female figure reclining either to the right or left with a child by her side, sometimes suckling her breast to the infant surrounded by a number of subordinate figures and a lady pressing her feet. Studies made earlier by the art historians on these sculptures suggest that such sculptures with Vaishnava affinities come from Central India (Pl. IC) while the Śaiva type enjoyed great popularity in Eastern India. The identification of the figures of the mother and child has long been a subject of debate, especially in the case of the stone sculptures of Bengal. In certain cases the issue was settled through the epigraphic evidence in the proper identification of a mother and child sculpture as Sadyōjāta Śiva. The mother and child stone sculptures with certain variations are well discussed and identified from various places such as

Dudhai (District Lalitpur, U.P.)[2], Sarya Buzurg (District Deoria, U.P.)[3], Verendi (Bengal)[4], Banswara (Rajasthan)[5], Khajuraho[6], Gwalior[7], Dhubela (M.P.)[8], Dinajpur (Burdwan University Museum)[9], Rajshahi District (National Museum, Delhi)[10] and Koshan Shahar (District Bogra, Bangla Desh).[11] While studying the iconography of these images scholars have identified them differently as pertaining to the various religious sects of Hinduism and non-Hindu religions and accordingly they were referred to as Krishna-Devaki,[12] Krishna-Yasoda[13], Sadyojata Mahesvara,[14] birth of Buddha, birth of a *mahāpuruṣa* or an emperor of great magnitude,[15] birth of Mahāvīra and Skandamātā.[16] N.P. Joshi has explained the reasons for the popularity of the stone sculptures of mother and child with the help of the statements furnished by the *Bhaviṣyad Purāṇa.*[17] He suggested that perhaps the belief that the worship of such slabs would dispel the fear of attack from outside as stated in *Bhaviṣyad Purāṇa* and that could be the reason for the occurrence of the stone slabs of mother and child theme in good numbers in India.

In this chapter an attempt has been made to analyse the iconography of one stone sculpture on a slab depicting the mother in reclining posture with her child lying by her side exhibited in the Indian Art Gallery of British Museum (OA 1872 7-1-107) with the identification as Yasoda suckling Kṛṣṇa. It measures approximately 6'x 4'. The sculptural panel depicts the figure of a mother reclining on her right side on the couch made of serpent coils with a child by her side suckling her breast and her right leg is slightly raised. Above her head, which is slightly elevated, is carved the five-hooded serpent *Śēṣa nāga* shielding her head in the manner of a canopy. The left hand of the mother that runs parallel to her body is broken. The left leg of the mother is slightly bent upwards being cared for by a lady attendant who is carved as two-handed. The head portion of the female attendant is broken. Above the sculpture are carved in two rows the images of the sages in seated posture, divine beings and flying *gandharvas* while the male attendants are carved to the right side of the slab. Below the bedstead are carved the seated images of the devotees in smaller proportions with their hands folded in *añjalī mudrā*. The figure of the mother is adequately decorated with long *hāras* dropping below the breasts, ear ornaments and anklets. The image of the mother demonstrates the heaviness of the body forms with her broad face and very large rounded breasts. This image of the mother nursing the baby gives an idea of the feeding practices which became almost a stereotyped pattern of showing the mother and child in Indian art. The associated figures carved on the top suggests that the child was born with the blessings of the divine beings. The stone slab of the mother and child from the British Museum can better be identified as Dēvakī Kṛṣṇa instead of Yaśōdā Kṛṣṇa as it is now being done and displayed in the sign board at the Museum. The reasoning that the image of the mother represents Yaśōdā cannot be accepted, as the real mother who gave birth to Kṛṣṇa was Dēvakī and not Yaśodā. Further as the mother is shown wearing a crown on her head, since she belongs to the royal family she may be considered as Dēvakī rather than Yaśodā who was the wife of Nanda, a landlord. The identification of the Mother and child slab from the British Museum as Dēvakī Kṛṣṇa and of its Vaiṣṇavite connection gains further support from the sculptural evidence of similar types of representations on the zoomorphic *Varāha mūrti* form reported from Badoh in Madhya Pradesh.[18] On the right side of the pedestal of the *Ādi Varāha* form has been carved the image of Dēvakī suckling Kṛṣṇa who is shown as lying on the *Śēṣa* bed. In the carving of the figures of Dēvakī Kṛṣṇa the artist sculptor has very carefully shown the *Śēṣa* hood behind the image of Kṛṣṇa to suggest that Kṛṣṇa is none other than the Supreme God himself. In these cases the mother can be identified as Dēvakī on the grounds of the textual reference to the birth of Kṛṣṇa in *Bhaviṣyad Purāṇa* and other texts. According to them lord Kṛṣṇa should be represented with an image of Dēvakī having just delivered the child on the couch.

They further describe that the child should be suckling her breast, while Lakṣmī should be shampooing her feet and the gods witnessing and rejoicing above in the air. A stone sculpture of the Mother and Child (Pl.IA) with the new born child on serpent bed with five planets shown on top and the seated figure of elephant-headed Gaṇēṣa being venerated by a female devotee has been described by C. Sivaramamurti in connection with the explanation of a *mahapurusha* for the new born child suggested by the exalted position of five planets.[19] In this connection, it is also mentioned that in several Pāla sculptures (Pl.IB) from Bihar and Bengal, there are all the nine planets shown and that only indicate that the child is born with the blessings of the nine planets favourably disposed to the new born, with no particular stress or indication as to the future of the child.[20]

Although the mother and child stone sculptures examined above displays the theme of the mother as reclining with the child by her side suckling the breast which became stereotyped, they form the primary source material for understanding the feeding activities of the newly born child and his close relations with the mother for the exploration of the dominant personality characteristics within the Hindu culture. For the crucial social interaction, through which an individual starts to separate himself and becomes a person, the infant needs his mother as a whole human being, not merely as a satisfier of hunger and thirst, or to state it more plainly what the infant requires is not a breast but a mother.[21] The significance of the portrayal of feeding the child by the mother should be viewed as a part of the total communication process in which not only the mother's breast but also the quality of her movement, caressing the child and touch affects the quality of the infant's sensory and emotional lease on life. It is rightly pointed out and shown by the anthropologists such as Kardiner, Benedict and Mead that the specific emotional colouring of many of a society's cultural institutions can directly be attributed to the dominant quality or mode of the first relationship, not in the sense of a simple casual connection, but in the complementarities and reciprocal influence between the mother-infant relations and other institutionalized forms of social relations.[22] It may be mentioned that here the breast can be viewed as a symbol for the mother, as feeding symbolizes the process of attachment in human development followed by the weaning process suggesting the separation of the mother and child, as the child grows. In Indian art, these aspects of nurturing the child by the mother (Fig.1A) and the childhood activities are very well demonstrated especially in the case of the image forms of Kṛṣṇa as a child (Bāla Kṛṣṇa) with his mother (Fig.1B).

Fig. 1A : Śiva, Pārvatī and Bāla Gaṇapati

Fig. 1B : Yaśoda Krṣna

The ideal mother is best illustrated in Hindu iconography through the images of *Saptamātrikas,* whose number is usually seven though eight or more of them can be counted.[23] In development of the iconography of the Seven Mothers it is observed that each of the mother holds a child in her left arm as it is noticed from a relief sculpture in the Mathura Museum.[24] In the Gupta sculpture displayed in Gwalior Museum are seen the examples of seven Mothers, each one with a child in her lap.[25] The *Saptamātrika* relief sculptures from Seraikela in the Singhbhum district now preserved in the Patna Museum represent the mother with a child on her left lap excepting *Varahi,* who has a small child seated between her legs.[26] The child seated on the lap of *Brāhmaṇī* is carved very realistically holding a toy in his left hand. The images of seven mothers at

Jaipur are all four-armed and each except *Chamunḍa* has a plump potbellied child on the left knee supported by the lower left hand.[27] Likewise, the Mārkaṇḍēśvara tank at Puri has five *Mātrika* figures, which are all four-armed supporting a child on their left thighs by their front left hands.

The images of *Yōginīs* are also found to carry a child on their laps being held by their left hands. It is interesting to observe a boar-faced child seated on the left lap of a *yōginī* called Umādevī who is shown as parrot-faced goddess.[28] In a *yōginī* temple at Lokhari in Banda district (U.P.) is noticed the image of a goddess *Hayagrīva* (horse-faced) who grazes upwards supporting a similarly horse-necked child on her left knee held by her left hand. She is shown as seated on a human corpse with a skullcap in her hand.[29] Another *yōginī* image kept in the Indian Museum called *Śrī Vasabha* is a bull-faced *yōginī* who supports on her knee a child with an elephant head.[30] The *yōginī* has bull mount and her attendants and worshippers shown below the image include an elephant headed female. Thus the images of *yōginīs* are carved with child being held close to their bodies which are shown sometimes with different heads as described above.

The preference to the male child in the patriarchal culture of Indian society is very much apparent from the classical literary texts of Hinduism. The Ṛg Vedic hymns are replete with prayers for sons and grandsons, male offerings, male descendants and male issues and occasionally for wives, but never for daughters. There were no signs of happiness or rejoicing over the birth of a daughter as it was in the case of the birth of a son.[31] The traditional preference for sons is found to be very much intact and the same has been reflected in the realm of art also. In the several images of Mother and Child described above, it is observed that in all cases they are the male children only. Further it is observed that in all the images the ideal mother is shown as displaying her affection, love and intimacy to the male child. The stone slabs of Dēvakī Kṛṣṇa are the best examples of the rejoicing that accompanied with the birth of a male child wherein the relief sculpture is beautifully carved with the figures of the several attendants and the divine beings including the image of goddess Lakṣmī who is shown as pressing the feet of Dēvakī, who just gave birth to Kṛṣṇa. Further it is observed that there is a consistent indication of marked preference for sons in the art forms that closely follows the iconographical and *Āgamic* textual descriptions. To understand the idea of parental love bestowed on the male child the sculptures of Sōmaskanda are excellent examples. They display the theme of parental love on the child who is often shown as seated in the middle of the seated images of Śiva and Pārvatī. In the Pallava stone sculptures and the bronzes of the Chola period Somaskanda is a favourite theme of the artists in which the child is shown in between suggesting that the object of love for both on the offspring has been bestowed entirely, which increases a thousand fold though given away in its entirety.[32]

The mother's nearness to the child may be viewed as an intense emotional involvement between the mother and child that plays an important role in an individual's personality formation through unconscious process. This aspect has been studied by Carstairs, who emphasizes the physical closeness between the Hindu mother and her child.[33] It is observed by him that the mother and child are seldom apart in the first two years and the baby is seen astride the mother's hip and the Hindu child has never been accustomed to frustration prior to weaning. Like Carstairs, Sudhir Kakar has broadly accepted the Hindu child's prolonged physical contact with the mother.[34] The psychoanalytical approach to study the sculptural data on physical contact between the mother and child in Hindu culture confirms the observational data presented by psychoanalysisist as evidence of sensual over-indulgence and of extreme emotional closeness in Hindu infancy. As the behaviour, the personality development, the attitudes of an individual towards women, sensuality, authority, power, non-violence and the Hindu view of the material world are all based on the childhood experiences, the symbolic representations of the mother-child in the Hindu iconography reveal a pattern which is highly meaningful.

References

1. Sigmund Freud., *An Outline of Psycho Analysis* 1940 (Standard Edition), Vol. 23, p. 188; John Boolby., "The Nature of the Child's Tie to His Mother", *International Journal of Psychoanalysis,* 39, 1958, pp. 350-373.
2. H.N. Singh, "Mother-Child Sculpture from Dudhai, District Lalitpur, Uttar Pradesh in *Indian Archaeological Heritage (Sh. K.V. Soundara Rajan Felicitation Volume)* ed. by C. Margabandhu et al., vol. II, Delhi, 1991, pp. 575-577.
3. *Ibid.*
4. N.K. Bhattasali., *Iconography of Buddhist and Brahmanical Sculptures in the Dacca Museum,* 1929.
5. R.C. Agrawal., "Krishna-Balarama in Rajasthan Sculptures and Epigraphs" *Indian Historial Quarterly,* XXV pp. 343-344.
6. U. Agarwal., *Khajuraho Sculpture and their Significance,* p. 81 fig. 59.
7. S.R. Thakore., *Catalogue of Sculptures in Archaeological Museum,* Gwalior, p. 13; A.K. Comaraswamy., *History of Indian and Indonesian Art,* pp. 86, 242 fig. 178.
8. S.K. Dikshit., *A Guide to State Museum,* Dhubela, pp. 28-29; pl. XII, XIII.
9. N.P. Joshi, "Puranas as Interpreters of Icons" in *Kala Journal of Indian Art History Congress*, vol. VII 2000-2001 ed. by Maruti Nandan Tiwari and Kamal Giri, Delhi, pp. 1-15.
10. V.S. Agrawala., *The Heritage of Indian Art,* Delhi, 1984, pl 70, p. 174.
11. *Ibid.*, Also see Susan L. Huntington., *The "Pala-Sena" Schools of Sculpture-Studies in South Asian Culture,* Institute of Asian Archaeology, Leiden, 1984 pl. 248, p. 185.
12. R. Awasthi., *Khajuraho Ki Deva Pratimayen* (Hindi) 1967, p. 115.
13. V.S. Agrawala, *op.cit.,* pl. 70, p. 174.
14. R.D. Banerji., *History of Bengal,* p. 256; N.K. Bhattasali., *op.cit.;* G. Bhattacharya., "The Munificence of lady Catuhsma", *Aksayanivi,* New Delhi, 1991, p. 317 ff.

15. C.Sivaramamurti., *Expressive Quality of Literary Flavour in Art,* Research Lectures, New Series 6, Dharwar, 1974, p.37, pl. XXIV.
16. Brijesh Krishna., *The Art Under Gurjara Pratiharas,* 1984, p. 170; pl. 81.
17. N.P. Joshi., *op.cit.,* p. 9; *Pujyate Pandavasresta janairutasavasamyutaih para cakrabhayam tatra na Kathapi bhavetpunah -- Bhavishya Purana* as cited by Vrataraja.
18. Haripriya Rangarajan., *Varaha Images in Madhya Pradesh - An Iconographial Study,* Delhi 1997, pp. 66-67, fig. 22.
19. C. Sivaramamurti., *op.cit.*
20. *Ibid.*
21. Sudhir Kakar., "Mother and Infants" In *The Essential Writings of Sudhir Kakar,* Delhi, 2001, p. 6.
22. *Ibid.*
23. A. Avalon., Introduction of *Prapanchasara Tantra,* p. 35; J.N. Banerjea, *Developemnt of Hindu Iconography,* p. 503.
24. V.S. Agrawala, *A Catalogue of the Brahmanical Images in Mathura Art,* p. 62, no. 552.
25. C. Sivaramamurti., *The Art of India,* New York, 1977, pp. 173-175.
26. Bhagawant Sahai., *Iconography of Minor Hindu and Budhist Deities,* Delhi, 1975, p. 207-219; *Journal of Oriental Institute* vol. XVIII, nos. 1 & 2, pp. 153-156, fig. 2-8.
27. *Memoirs of Archaeological Survey of India,* 42, pp. 3 and 18.
28. Vidya Dehejia., *Yogini Cult and Temples - A Tantric Tradition,* Delhi, 1986, p. 146.
29. *Ibid.,* p. 159.
30. *Ibid.,* p. 168.
31. A.A. Mac Donell., *Vedic Religion,* p. 165 quoted in R.M. Das, *Women in Manu and His Seven Commentators,* Varanasi, 1962, p. 43.
32. C. Sivaramamurti., *op.cit.,* pp. 30-31.
33. Carstairs G. Morris., *The Twice Born: A Study of A Community of High Caste Hindus,* Bloomington, 1967, pp. 63-76; 157.
34. Sudhir Kakar., *The Inner World: A Psycho Analytic Study of Childhood and Society in India,* Delhi, 1978, p. 193; T.G. Vaidyanathan & Jeffrey J Kripal, ed. *Vishnu on Freud's Desk : A Reader in Psychoanalysis and Hinduism,* Delhi, 1999, pp. 185-216.

Section - II

Tantrism-Tantra in Art, Architecture and Culture

6

Iconography of the Tantric Goddess Chinnamastā and Human Sacrifices

The Tantric goddess *Chinnamastā* is mentioned as one of the *Mahāvidyas* in the Hindu *Tantric* texts that has its parallels in the *Tantric* Buddhist iconography as *Chinnamuṇḍā, Vajra Vārāhī or Chakrasambara.* In the present chapter an attempt has been made to discuss the plausible explanations and meanings of the iconographic, *tantric* and religious symbolism of the goddess. It also highlights the violent cum erotic character of *Chinnamastā* in relation to the blood sacrifice and human sacrifices mentioned in the *Kālikā Purāṇa* and the sculptural relief works of self-immolation noticed in the temples of *Chāmuṇḍā* and *Bhairava* at Bhubanesvar, Tripurantakam (A.P.) and the construction of temples and *maṇḍapas* specifically for the purpose of head-offering as referred to in the medieval Telugu literature. It is also intended to examine the eyewitness accounts left by the foreign travellers in this connection and the head-hunting practices associated with the fertility rites observed in Indonesia to present rationalized views on the self-decapitation, drinking of one's own blood and the violence demonstrated by the *Tantric* goddess and the gruesome practices of human sacrifices during the medieval times.

Paintings and sculptures of *Chinnamastā, a Tantric* goddess, seems to be of fairly recent origin. The images of *Chinnamastā* are found among the series of miniatures with the ten *Mahāvidyās* produced by the Pahari and Rajput schools, on drawings and paintings from Rajasthan, on folk paintings from Kalighat (Fig. 1C, 1D) and the model books from Nepal

Fig 1C

Fig 1D : *Chinnamastā*

datable to 18th century.[1] However the *Chinnamastā* figures are likely to have existed among the miniature paintings of the early Basohli and Kangra schools in the 16th century.[2] In the stone media the figures of *Chinnamastā* have been reported from the late Hinḍu temples in the North East of India and in Nepal, the oldest datable to the middle of seventeenth century A.D. In Orissa, a sixteenth century Chaṇḍī temple had the earliest Hindu image of *Chinnamastā*. While discussing the iconographical features of the image it has been suggested by Thomas E Donaldson that this figure is probably based on painting rather than on temple sculpture.[3] The relief represents the goddess assuming a walking posture, while standing on a lotus. She is naked with dishevelled hair, wears the usual ornaments among which is a garland of skulls and holds her severed head in her left hand. She holds a sword in her right hand while three streams of blood spring from her throat and are drunk by herself and her two attendants. The female attendants hold each a sword and a skull bowl in their hands. The image is without the erotic couple below. Since the relief belongs to a temple for the goddess *Chaṇḍī* that contains several erotic scenes and erotic imagery it can be suggested that they have substituted the purpose of the erotic figures below the figure of *Chinnamastā.*[4]

Tantrasāra quotes two lists of *Mahāvidyās* from *Mālinīvijaya* and *Muṇḍamāla* in which *Chinnamastā* has figured as a goddess. The list cited from *Tantrasāra* is attributed to *Chāmuṇḍa* Tantra and *Śabdakalpadruma*. The same has been mentioned in *Tantra Kaumudi,*[5] which contains two lists of *Mahāvidyās* of which one list contains 27, while the other one gives the number of the goddesses as 10. Like the other goddesses such as *Prachaṇḍa Chaṇḍikā, Uchchiṣṭa Chaṇḍālinī, Dhūmavatī, Vāgala, Vāgalāmukhī, Pitā and Karṇa Piśāchi, Chinnamastā* is worshipped with the ulterior motives of securing magical powers. These goddesses have fearful appearances and have very few regular worshippers, who have them as their tutelary deities. In the *Tantra* literature it is mentioned that *Chinnamastā* holds by her left hand her severed head from her body, while the head and two female deities stand by her sides drinking streams of blood flowing from the headless trunk. She stands on *Rati* and *Kāmadēva* who are engaged in *Viparīta rati*. She looks like a girl of sixteen and has highly developed breasts.[6] In the *Mahānirvāṇa Tantra* the goddess *Chinnamastā* is stated as the goddess of *rajas* quality and that it bestows minor liberations like wealth, heaven, etc., who is invoked especially in connection with *ṣaṭkarmas* and allied purposes. In the *Tantric* cult practices of *Chinnamastā* the male deity, the *Bhairava,* has an unique place and he is mentioned as *Vikarialka.*[7]

In the *Praṇatōṣinī Tantra* the origin of *Chinnamastā* is described in a detailed manner. According to it, *Pārvatī* went to bathe in the *Mandākinī* river along with her attendants *Jaya* and *Vijaya* and, after completing the bathing, the goddess's colour became black as she was sexually aroused. When her two attendants asked her for food as they were feeling very hungry she said that she would give them the food but they have to wait for it for a while, as she was thinking about some matters at that time. After some time the two atendants pleaded her once again for food as they were her children and that she should provide food and clothing for them as their mother and praised her by stating that she is well-known for her nature of mercy. Then once again the goddess, the consort of Śiva told them that she would give them anything only after she reached her home. The two attendants again begged her for food and boons to fulfil their desires. On hearing this merciful goddess smiled and severed her head and the head fell on the palm of her left hand. From her throat sprung three streams of blood, one to the left and one to the right that fell respectively into the mouths of her flanking attendants and the centre one fell into her mouth. After performing this all were satisfied and later returned home.[8]

In the *Tantric* Buddhist art one can find the parallel image for *Chinnamastā* who is known as *Chinnamuṇḍā, Vajra Vārāhī* or the Yellow *Vajra Yōginī. Vajra Yōginī* is another *Śakti* of *Hēruka* and this goddess is shown as being either red or yellow in colour, standing in *ālīḍha*, carrying her own severed head in her upraised left hand and *kartarī* in her right hand. Vajra Yōginī is identical in appearance with the *Śakta* goddess *Chinnamastā*. Generally, she is represented as accompanied by two *Yōginīs,* one on either side of her. A miniature painting from Nepal shows the goddess Vajra Yōginī as closely resembling the Kangra miniature painting of *Chinnamastā.*[9] The decapitated goddess *Vajrayōgini* accomapanied by her two attendants is standing on a pair of subjugated deities engaged in sexual intercourse in a reverse position. In the Buddhist context the pair of subjugated deities are identified as *Bhairava* and *Kālarātri* and not as *Kāma* and *Rati*. The importance of this miniature painting of Nepal is that so far it is the only Buddhist example of *Chinnamuṇḍā* trampling a pair of deities. In *Sādhanamāla* the iconographical features of *Chinnamuṇḍā* are described under the name of *Vajra Yōginī* that includes the motifs of self-decapitation and the flowing of three streams of blood. The images of *Vajra Yōginī* can hardly be distinguished from *Vajra Vārāhī*.[10] *Vajra Vārāhī* stands for at least seven varieties of a gruesome, bloodthirsty goddess who herself is associated with the equally terrifying male deities *Hēruka/ Hēvajra* and *Chakra Sambara*.

In explaining the function and religious meanings of the *tantric* goddess *Chinnamastā* images, a distinction could be made between the Hindu and Buddhist traditions and the specific *Tantric* schools within them. In the *Tantrasāra* of 16th century the cosmic associations are mentioned for the images and it is stated that the goddess is venerated in rites that should destroy the enemies and in the rites of revenge.[11] While interpreting the meanings of the motifs displayed in this image the art historians have emphasised the self-sacrificing and nourishing intent of *Chinnamastā*. It is further explained that the obvious implication in this kind of imagery is of primal sacrifice and renewal of creation. The goddess sacrifices herself and her blood, drunk by her attendants, renews or resuscitates the Universe. Therefore, beheading her own head is a temporary expedient to provide food and appears to be a more sanguinary manifestation of the goddess as *Shākāṁbharī* and *Annapūrṇa*. From the ritualistic aspect it is observed from the *Tantra* text *Śaktisangama Tantra* that the goddess *Chinnamastā* is very fond of *Vāmāchāra* traditions that involve the offerings of blood and *pañchamakaras*.[12]

The story of the origin of the goddess has been explained as she is the *Śakti* by which the Great Mother sacrifices herself for the happiness of her children who virtually sucks the life blood of the Mother. She serves herself in her love for the children and feeds them with her own blood. The transcendental power of will and vision are well documented in the iconology of *Chinnamastā*. Both the destructive and creative aspects are shown in the form of severing her own head and she signifies apparent dissolution and return to the elements and reconstitution into other forms. Thus the process of being is an unbroken and infinite one. The figures of Rati and Kāma in erotic posture demonstrate the union the of male and female principles as a symbol of eternal communion and an awareness of oneness through duality.[13] The third eye of *Chinnamastā* looks beyond space and time. She is the changeless, limitless primordial power and is without any beginning or end. Her nakedness symbolizes creation; her full and high breasts denote preservation and her true nature stands for eternal liberation.

The iconographical composition of the figure of *Chinnamastā* reminds us of the esoteric ritual practices, the ritual head-hunting practices and the taking or borrowing of a head in the genesis of *Gaṇēśa* followed in parts of South East Asia that got its development in the remote past from the Indian inspiration and transformed to strengthen the indigenous needs and beliefs. In some tribal areas of South East Asia, at harvest feast, the ancestors for supplying them with heads bless the men headhunters with good crops and health.[14] The ritual practice of killing a human being as an offering to the deity can be noticed from the type of images from Sahdol, Bheraghat, Ranipur Jharial and Rikhiyan.[15] In them the images of *yōginīs* are found with corpses, severed human heads, skull cups and curved *kartari* knives. *Vārāhī Tantra* mentions the extraordinary group of yōginīs (*vichitra yōginī gaṇa*) established among headless bodies and severed heads (*ruṇḍa muṇḍa paristhite*)[16] It is evident from the depiction of *yōginis* with severed heads in their hands that the esoteric rituals of the *yōginis* involve human sacrifice, particularly the head offering which can be connected with the imagery of *Chinnamastā* that displays the self-decapitation of the head and drinking of blood. The demonstration of sacrificial violence by the *Chinnamastā* can be compared to the sacrificial act of a devotee for fulfilling a vow or to attain some supernatural powers or a warrior who offers his own head for the sake of victory. As *Chinnamastā* is considered as one of the *Mahāvidyās* embodied with deified spell she is worshipped in that form either to ensure success in their lives or for a guaranteed victory.

The description given in the *Sādhanamāla* of 9th century A.D. with regard to *Chinnamuṇḍā* meditation reveals the association between the three arteries of the yōga body and the concepts of wisdom, means and the thought of enlightenment in a rather formal way while it emphasizes the result of the meditation on this goddess and of the recitation of her *mantra,* conquering obstacles, winning women and terrifying cities and kings.[17] Whether Hindu or Buddhist, the aims of the *tantric* rites are not very different and the *Chinnamastā* belongs to the group of terrifying goddesses, *Mahāvidyās.* They are known as the Great Spells with their supernatural powers and helps the devotees in conquering enemies and in fulfilling their desires. By the aggressive appearance both *Chinnamastā* and *Chinnamuṇḍā* are blood-thirsty goddesses and can be related to the practice of self-decapitation that existed in South India during the early Pallava and Chōla periods as is evident from the several Pallava panels, where the devotee is shown as offering his own head. Further a late Pallava inscription on a slab refers to a warrior who had offered his own head to the Goddess and the stone slab itself contains a relief of that act.[18] The practice of self-immolation in Andhra during medieval times is also known from the sculptural slabs found at Tripurantakam. The Śiva temple at Śrisailam had a *maṇḍapa* hall meant for the practice of self-immolation and it is mentioned as *Vīra śirōmaṇḍapa.* Further in some of the *Śakti* temples of Andhra region human sacrifices have been offered on the altars and this is mentioned in *Siṁhāsana Dvātriṁśika*. Therein such temples were mentioned as *Chaṁpuḍu guḷḷu*. In Orissa, self-decapitation is recorded in sculptural relief works of Vaital Deul where *Chāmuṇḍa* and *Bhairava* are worshipped. Vidya Dehejia mentions a *Bhairava* image in which a severed human head is depicted lying beside the god, while two more severed heads are carved on a tripod depicted below the image.[19] In the Hindu iconography such scenes of violence, beheading by means of sword and trampling the enemies can be found in the imagery of *Bhairava*, *Mahishāsura mardinī*, Śiva as *Śarbhēśa mūrti* - *Gajāsura*, *Andhakāsura saṁhāramūrti* and *Brahma Śiraschēdaka*, *Natarāja mūrti* and *Nirṛiti*. For the textual reference to the blood sacrifice and even human sacrifice, can be cited the elaborate descriptions given in the *Kālikā Purāṇa* datable to 11th century A.D.[20] In the work are mentiond rituals of blood from one's throat or pieces of one's own flesh or even one's own body. It is stated in the work that a worshipper who offers his flesh and blood from eight parts of his body will obtain the destruction of enemies and the human sacrifice made to the goddess is considered as an exceedingly great obligation.[21]

In the observations recorded by Abbe Dubois also there is reference to the human and animal sacrifices offered to the goddesses.[22] It is mentioned that *naramēdha* or human sacrifice is held to be infinitely more pleasing to the deity, who is the object of the ceremony. In the eyewitness account given by him it is mentioned that he had visited several places where the scenes of carnage used to be enacted.

Thus the inner and international meaning of the scenes of self-sacrifice and drinking of blood displayed in the iconography of *Chinnamastā* has been demonstrated through the archaeological and literary sources discussed above. From the *Tantric* point of view, *Chinnamastā,* one of the *Mahāvidyās,* embodies the deified spell, which ensures success to the worshipper. The worshipping of the powerful *Tantric* Goddess *Chinnamastā* in *Vāmāchāra* practice reveals the long tradition that involves the self-sacrifice and blood offerings that spread over a large area of the Indian subcontinent from North to South.

References

1. Ph Rawson., *Tantra Catalogue, London Arts Council of Great Britain,* 1971, fig 211-219; E Beuard., *Chinnamastā, The Awful Buddhist and Hindu Tantric Goddess*-Buddhist Tradition Series, vol. 22, Delhi, 1994; M.L.B. Blom., *Depicted Deities, Painters' Model Books in Nepal,* Ph.D Dissertation, Utrecht University, 1989, pp. 54-56.
2. B.N. Goswamy and Klaus Fischer., *Pahari Meister,* Zurich, 1990, p. 31.
3. Thomas E Donaldson., *Hindu Temple Art of Orissa, Studies in South Asian Culture* vol XII, Leiden 1986, p. 742, fig. 1827.
4. Karel R vankooji., "Iconography of the Battlefield: the case of Chinnamasta" in *Violence, Denied Violence, Non-violence and the Rationalization of Violence in South Asian Cultural History* ed. By Houben & Karel R vankooji, Leiden, 1999, pp. 249-274.
5. Chintamani Chakravarty., *The Tantra-Studies on Their Religion and Literature,* Calcutta, 1963, pp. 85-88; N.N. Bhattacharya., *History of the Tantric Religion. An Historical, Ritualistic and Philosophical Study*, Delhi 1999, Second edition, revised. 325; D.N. Bose., *Tantras: Their Philosophy and Occult Secrets,* Calcutta, 3rd edition enlarged, 1956.
6. N.N. Bhattacharya, *op.cit.,* p. 325.
7. *Ibid.,* p. 328.
8. Pratapaditya Pal., *Hindu Religion and Iconology According to Tantrasara,* Los Angels, 1981; David Kinsley., *Tantric Visions of the Divine Feminine,* New Delhi, 1998.
9. M. Th. Mallmann., *Introduction a l'Iconographie du Tantrisme Bouddhique, Biblioteque du center de recherches sur l'Asie Centrale et la Haue Asie* vol. I Paris, 1975; pl. XII, 2.
10. *Ibid.,* p. 432.
11. Pratapaditya Pal., *op.cit.,* p. 316.
12. N.N. Bhattacharya., *op.cit.,* p. 316.
13. T.N. Misra., *Impact of Tantra on Religion and Art,* Delhi, 1997, p. 12-13.

14. R.E. Downs., "Head Hunting in Indonesia", *Structural Anthropology in the Netherlands* ed. By P.E. De Josselin de Jong The Hague, 1977 p. 123.
15. Vidya Dehejia., *Yogini Cult and Temples - A Tantric Tradition,* Delhi, 1986 p. 58.
16. *Varahi Tantra* ed. by Buddhisagar Sharman, 1964, vol 3 p. 139.
17. M. Nihom., "The Goddess with Severed Head : A Recession of Sādhanamāla 232, 234 and 238 attributed to the Siddhacharya Virupa" in : *Ritual, State and History in South Asia,* Essays in Honour of Heesterman, eds. A.W. van der Hoek, Leiden, 1992 p. 222-243.
18. *S.I.I.* vol. XII No 106. Also see N.N. Bhattacharya., *op.cit.*, p. 353.
19. Vidya Dehejia., *Early Stone Temples of Orissa,* Delhi, 1979, p. 12-13.
20. Karel R van Kooij., *Worship of the Goddess According to the Kālikā Purāṇa,* Part I, Orientalia Rheno Traiectina, vol. XIV, Leiden, 1972, p. 3.
21. *Ibid.*, pp. 52-53.
22. Abbe Dubois., *Hindu Manners, Customs and Ceremonies,* Oxford, First edition, 1897, pp. 646.

7

Tantric Temples of Śakti Deities in Modern Times

The *Tantric* ideas and practices have found most favourable ground for their meaningful survival and development in the *Śākta* religion. The most notable feature of the *Śākta Tantric* idea is that the Supreme Being is female which is worshipped under different names and forms. Unlike in other religious systems where the position of the goddess is conceived of as the wife of the male god, she is conceived of as the inherent *Śakti* of the male god, inseparable from his own entity or self in the Sakta religion where the Tantric influence is greater. But the *Tantric* rituals and practices followed in the worship of the *dēvī,* in course of time, came in for severe criticism and were often decried as ridiculous and detestable due to the involvement of blood, human sacrifices besides the offering of *pañcha makaras (madya, māṁsa, matsya, mudra and maithuna)*. Such conclusions seem to have been made due to the misconceptions of the subject and the imperfect understanding of the mystic and esoteric elements in *Tantrism*. Further, it can also be attributed to the fact that the vast literature on *Tantra* remained the preserve of a small group of *sādhakas* (initiated persons) and learned men and that attempts were not undertaken to publicise the concepts, philosophy, religious meanings and the essence of the *Tantric* rituals and practices among the common people. Therefore, an attempt has been made in the present paper to describe the art, architecture and rituals observed in the *Tantric* temples dedicated to the goddesses of the medieval times and to compare them with the *Śrī Chakra* temple of Devipuram for the better appreciation of and understanding of the socio-religious significance of the *Tantric* temples of *Śakta* faith through the ages. It is intended to present a critical, objective and dispassionate analysis of the *Tantric* techniques, rituals and practices followed in such temples on the basis of the references contained in the literary sources, inscriptions of the medieval times, the personal observations and interviews conducted with the *sādhakas* of the temple at Devipuram. Besides its descriptive and comparative intent, it is also aimed to make a psychological enquiry into the intimate connection between mental illness and society, as it would reveal certain social values and pressures operating within the Indian society in the process of several healing traditions and *Tantric* practices followed. It is observed that the *Tantric* practices combine elements from classical Indian astrology, medicine, alchemy and magic spells with beliefs and practices drawn from the folk and popular traditions.

Tantricism was concentrated during the medieval period and the first Brahmanical *tantric pīṭha* was developed in Odra *dēśa* and the presiding deity was lord Jagannath and Kātyāyanī was the goddess.[1] During the period from 8th to 12th centuries A.D. the circular 64 *yōginī* temples of *Śākta-tantric* cult were constructed and these were concentrated mostly in Central and Eastern India. The architectural feature that distinguishes these *Yōginī* temples from the other Hindu temples is their circular shape not covered by any roof. So far no *śilpaśāstra* pertaining to the architecture of the hypaethral temples has been found and these temples are basically different from the Brahmanical and other Hindu shrines. Likewise, they are also not similar in architecture to any known Buddhist monuments and thereby form a distinct style. Art historians have explained the feature of the circular architectural plan in terms of *maṇḍala, yantra* or *chakra* being used most prominently in the *tantric* cult practices. *Maṇḍala* is used in the sense of a circle and is referred to in *Matsya Purāṇa* as is drawn with powders of five colours. *Agnipurāṇa* also refers to eight *maṇḍalas* including *sarvatōbhadra* and others. The *chakra* or the circle may represent the principle that has no beginning and end but is perfectly symmetrical.[2] The *Yōginis* in circular temple might represent such unending principle or *maṇḍala*. *Śrī Chakra,* the form of supreme *Śakti* and *Śiva*, together is verily the macrocosm as well as the microcosm i.e., the body of two in one, *Śiva-Śakti*. *Yantra* which is sometimes known as *chakra* is a diagram engraved or drawn on different materials and resembles the *maṇḍala,* but the difference between them is that *yantra* is specially appropriated to the worship of a particular deity, while the *maṇḍala* may be employed for the worship of any deity. The well-known temples of 64 *yōginīs* located at Hirapur, Ranipur Jharial, Lalitpur, Dhudhai, Bheraghat and Khajuraho display the common architectural feature of the circular shrine with niches to accommodate the images of the *Yōginīs* either seated or standing and a *maṇḍapa* in front. At Khajuraho there is a central temple and surrounding walls with 64 small cells. While a passage is constructed for the *Yōginī* temple at Hirapur, it is absent at Ranipur Jharial and the circular shrine contains 64 niches with a *maṇḍapa* in the centre of the circular enclosure to enshrine the image of dancing Śiva. The sixty-four *Yōginī* temples at Bheraghat have the circular cloister and it is observed that the present structure is the work of two different periods. The original structure consisting of the circular wall built in 10th century with its inscribed statues while the pillared cloister with its roof was the work of 12th century A.D. The original *Śākta pīṭhas* are not associated with any erotic imagery or sexual display. This could be attributed to the reason that the basic tenet of *Tantra* is not to expose their practices to the uninitiated and they conduct everything in strict secrecy.

Although the ground plan and the elevation of the *Yōginī* temples differ from the other Hindu temples, the most important part of the temple is the *garbha* (womb) as the name describes it perfectly. The god in the form of the chief idol is placed in the womb heading up to the *garbha* from the porch is a kind of corridor through which one enters.[3] The Rājārāṇi temple at Bhuvaneswar as a Manjusri type of temple based on the *Śrī Chakra* or *Śrī Yantra* was described by Bettina Baumer.[4] It is of interest to mention here the story of building a beautiful town of Vijayanagara (Vidyānagara) in imitation of the mystic *Śrī Chakra* by the author of Vidyārṇava, when he acted as a regent in pursuance of the wishes of the people on the death of king Praudha Dēva who died leaving the queen with child.[5] Although it may not be historical, it is important for its reference to the mystic diagram *Śrī Chakra*.

In the modern times a *Tantric* temple has been constructed in Hooghley district in West Bengal, 50 km away from Calcutta in Eastern India. The temple named as Hamsēśvari is a six-storeyed temple built in the *manḍala* pattern of *sarvatōbhadra* type.[6] Except these few references to the architectural plans of the *Tantric* temples not much is known about the use of either *Śrī Chakra* or any other *yantra* or *manḍala* for the ground plan and the elevation of the temples from Indian context. But quite interestingly, *Śrī Chakra* has been chosen not only for the ground plan but also for the elevation of a modern temple built at Devipuram near Anakapalle (A.P.) (Pl. IIA & B) for the goddess *Tripurasundarī,* one of the *tantric* goddesses, categorized under *Mahā Vidyas*.[7] It is also associated with a *Kāmākhya* and a Śiva temple. The temple stands almost unparalleled in Andhra. It has a beauty of its own, which is not to be found in any other shrine. It is a three-storeyed temple in *Śri Chakra* design with 108' length, 108' breadth and 54' height. It is in reality a glorious specimen of the wondrous achievement of the architectural art. The plan of the temple and the icons installed in it were entirely the conception of Sri Amritananda Natha, who is a *sādhaka* and *guru* of *Śri Vidyā* practice. His intention and purpose is mainly to demonstrate through this temple the essence of *Śrī Vidyā,* which leads to a total independence called liberation to all the people without any distinction of race, religion, caste or colour. The temple is beautifully decorated with 108 icons of the *dēvī* images, with their names inscribed and made in *aṣṭaṭala* measurement in seated posture with a small pedestal in front of each image with *Śrī Chakra Yantra* drawn on top of them to facilitate the devotees to perform the rituals.

The iconography of the 108 *dēvī* images of the temples is not strictly in accordance with any of the descriptions known from the *Śilpa* texts and the inclusion of these deities and their names are drawn purely from the *Khaḍgamāla* of *Śri Lalitā Sahasranāma Stōtram*. The iconographical features of the images i.e., the number of arms, the weapons and attributes held in their hands, were all drawn from the inspiration and devotional faith of the founder of the temple. The nomenclature of the *yōginīs* and *Śākta tantric* deities mentioned in the different *Purāṇas* and *Tantric* texts such as *Kālikā Purāṇa, Skanda Purāṇa, Bṛiha Nīlā Tantra* is found to be different from the one given in the *Khaḍgamāla*. Interestingly it agrees with a list of *yōginīs* enumerated as many as sixty-nine grouped into eight categories mentioned in *Śrītattvanidhi.*[8] According to this text the *yōginīs* were categorized as *Prakaṭa Yoginis* (11), *Gupta Yōginis* (16), *Guptatara Yōginis* (8), *Sampradāya Yōginis* (12), *Kulōttīrna Yōginis* (10), *Nigarbha Yōginis* (10), *Rahasya Yōginis* (8) and *Atirahasya Yōginis* (3). The iconographical details and the names of the *yōginis* categoried under these groups mentioned in *Khaḍgamāla* are given in tables based on the descriptions furnished in *Śrītattvanidhi*.

The *Śrī Chakra* or *Śrī Yantra* or *Tripurā Chakra* chosen for the temple design is the most important *Tantric* diagram connected with the cult of *Śri Vidyā.* The diagram symbolizes the body of the goddess. According to the descriptions given in *Nityaṣōdasīkārṇava*[9] and *Kāmakaḷā* Vilāsa,[10] it consists of 9 triangles or *yōnis,* of which five of them are in the name of

Śakti and four in that of Śiva. In *Soundaryalahari* also it is mentioned that the *Śakti* triangles are pointed upwards and the *Śiva* triangles downwards.[11] The images of the goddesses mentioned above and a few more images are placed in nine enclosures of *Śrī Chakra* temple. The main goddess *Lalitā* is shown as seated in *ardhaparyaṅka* pose with her right leg folded and left one dangling down. The image of *Sadāśiva* in reclining posture is shown beneath her. The *Sadāśiva* image below the goddess reminds us of the form of the union known as *Yuganaddha* in which the Male principle is shown in union with the Female principle, a theme very often represented in *Tantric* Buddhist art.[12] It reflects the non-dual state of unity of *śūnyatā* and *karuṇa*.[13] *Sri Vidyā* or *Tripurā* or *Tripurasundarī* or *Lalitā* is also known by the name *Ṣōḍasī* and is an important goddess of the group of *Mahā Vidya* goddesses according to the *Tantric* texts. In them she is conceived of as a very beautiful and youthful damsel. Her nature is benign and she has to be installed on a red lotus and she should also be shown in red garments. She should be endowed with four hands and three eyes. Here at Devipuram interestingly the goddess is shown in benign form decorated adequately with four hands carrying *śankha,* sugar cane and flowers.

The ritual practices followed at this temple include the worship of Divine Mother Lalithā (Fig. 2A) with intimate services. It means the worship of the Goddess within, with the awareness in the body and for this purpose the living men and women who have the characteristics of Śiva and *Śakti* are worshipped as the best forms of *Śrī Chakra* and is generally referred to as *Suvāsinī pūja*.[14] The external worship of the living woman as the embodiment of the goddess pleases her and it will be followed by an internalization of this form of worship within them. For the realization of *sāmarasya* or equilibrium of *Śiva-Śakti* within his own self the person initiated in this *Śrī Vidyā* system has to perform certain secret rites. In the performance of rituals, it is observed that *Vajra Pañjara Nyāsa* forms an integral part. *Nyāsa* is an important method of

Tantric worship, which consists of feeling the god in different parts of the body. It is the imaginary placing of different objects on different parts of the body with which the aspirant invokes

Sri Sahashrakshi Raja Rajeswari, Devipuram

Fig. 2A : Main Deity, Devipuram

the god to come and occupy certain parts of his body. It is done by touching the chest and limbs with the tips of the fingers and the palm of the right hand accompanied by *mantrās*.[15] In the ritual practices followed, there do not seem to be any distinction between the worshipper and the worshipped. Not only the worship but also the repetition of *mantras* and recitation of the thousand names of the Goddess form an important part for the devotees of *Śrī Vidyā*. By uttering the *bīja mantrās* the *Kuṇḍalinī Śakti* wll be aroused for the fulfillment of the desires of the devotees. While describing the effects of *Śrī Vidyā mantra* Kulārṇava says that the *mantra* saves the aspirants from all sorts of danger.[16] According to Jñanārṇava, millions of *Vājapēyas* and thousands of *aśvamēdhas* and even gifts of crores of *kapila* cows are not equal in merit to the *Śri Vidyā mantra*.[17] The *Śri Vidyā* school has an extensive literature of its own and it claims Agastya, Durvāsa and Dattātrēya as its earlier exponents. Of them mention may be made of *Śrī Vidyā Nitya Pūjā Paddhati*, a ritualistic work dealing with the details of the worship of *Tripurā*.[18]

From the brief descriptive account given on the *Śrī Chakra* temple at Devipuram with regard to its architectural design, ritual practices and the concept of worshipping the living male and females in the back-drop of the historical account of the Śakti temples meant for the worship of the *Yōginīs* and the *Śākta Tāntric* goddesses, it is evident that the *Tāntric* rituals and practices which were widely practised with the involvement of *pañcha makaras* and other revolting practices of the earlier times were not being followed in the modern *Tāntric* temple under study. It is also observed from the field study that absolutely allegorical and yōgic interpretations were sometimes given to these rites and that the *yantra, mantra, nyāsa* and *mudras* form the main components in the adoration of *Śakti* and *Śiva* who are shown in the *yuganaddha* form. Another important aspect of the ritual traditions followed at this temple is the *Suvāsinis,* who perform the *Śrī Chakra pūja* after their initiation under the *sadhakas*. From the historical accounts drawn from the literary works such as *Yaśastilaka* of Sōmadēva Sūri and *Simhāsana Dvātrimśika* of Koravi Goparaju we could get the picture of the *Śākta Tāntric* deities as horrid places frequented by the terrible female spirits known as *Mahāyōginis*

Table Showing the List of Names of the Goddesses Under Various Groups Based on Śrī Tattvanidhi

Prakaṭa yōginīs	Gupta yōginīs	Guptatara yōginīs	Sampradāya yōginīs	Kulōttīrna yōginīs	Nigarbha yōginīs	Rahasya yōginīs	Ati Rahasya yōginīs
Sarva Saṁkshōbhiṇi	*Kāmākarshiṇī*	*Anaṅga Kusumā*	*Sarva Vidrāvaṇī*	*Sarvasiddhipradā*	*Sarvajña*	*Vāsinī*	*Kāmēśvarī*
Sarva Vidrāvaṇī	*Buddhyākarshiṇī*	*Ananga Mēkhala*	*Sarvākarshiṇī*	*Sarva Sampratpradā*	*Sarvaśaktī*	*Kāmesvarī*	*Vajrēsvarī*
Sarvākarshiṇī	*Adhaṁkārākarshiṇī*	*Anangamadanā*	*Sarvāhlādinī*	*Sarvapriyaṁkarī*	*Sarvaiśvarya pradāyinī*	*Mōdinī*	*Bhagamālini*
Sarvavaśaṁkarī	*Śabdākarshiṇī*	*Anangamadanātura*	*Sarvasammōhinī*	*Sarvamaṅgaḷākārinī*	*Sarvajñamayī*	*Vimalā*	
Sarvōnmādinī	*Sparśākarshiṇī*	*Anangarēkha*	*Sarvasthaṁbhinī*	*Sarvakāmapradā*	*Sarvarakshā SarvaRūpiṇī*	*Aruṇā*	
Sarvamahāṁkuśī	*Rūpākarshiṇī*	*Anangavēginī*	*Sarvajhṛiṁbhiṇī*	*Sarva dukha vimōchanī*	*Sarvepsita phalapradā*	*Jāyanī*	
Sarva Khechari	*Rasakarshini*	*Anangamkusa*	*Sarva Vasamkari*	*Sarva Mrityu Prasamani*		*Sarvesvari*	
Sarva bījā	*Gandhākarshiṇī*	*Anangamālini*	*Sarvaranjanī*	*Sarva Vighnakāriṇī*		*Kaulinī*	
Sarva Yōnī	*Chittākarshiṇī*	*Sarva Saṁkshōbhiṇī*	*Sarvōnmādinī*	*Sarvajña Sundarī*			
Sarva Trikhaṇḍā	*Dhariyākarshiṇī*		*Sarvārdha Sādhikē*				
Trailōkya Mōhanā	*Smṛityākarshiṇī*		*Sarva Sampattipūriṇī*				
	Nāmākarshiṇī		*Sarva mantramayī*				
	Bījākarshiñī		*Sarvadvaṁdaśaṁkarī*				
	Ātmākarshiṇī		*Sarva Saubhāgyadāyakī*				

and a crowd of fanatical votaries, engaged in outrageous forms of self torture.[19] The offering of blood sacrifices and human sacrifices are referred to in the Telugu literary works of Koravi Goparaju in which they are mentioned as *Chaṁpudu guḷḷu.*[20] Information of similar nature can also be gathered from the eyewitness account given by Abbe Dubois.[21] It may be mentioned here that the practices of offering flesh, blood or human beings all depended on the nature and philosophy of different Tāntric traditions and, therefore, such practices are not to be seen in the *Śrī Vidyā Tāntric* tradition followed at Devipuram. This kind of transformation in the *Tāntric* ritual practices from the extremely vulgar and anti-religious rites that rouse the contempt of the people at large not only for the practitioners but for the *Tantra* system of religion as a whole to that of the *Tantric* practices, aimed at complete self-control and worshipping of the goddess through external and internal process to visualise the goddess within one's own Self can be attributed not only to the different *tāntric* traditions but also to keep pace with the social acceptability, the changing ideology and attitude of the people of modern times.

The mental healing and soothing offered to many of the devotees through this kind of *Tāntric* tradition cannot totally be ignored. The mystical spiritual traditions of the *Tāntric* religion are rendering great service to human beings by way of consoling the affected souls and providing a path for regulating the individual self by aiming a more *dhārmic* way of life leading to the restoration of moral and spiritual well-being. From the personal interview that we had with Dr. Amritananda Natha a renowned scientist in Nuclear Physics and a *Śri Vidyā* practitioner, it is noticed that so far he initiated approximately 2,000 people into *Śrī Chakra* worship, which resulted in bringing success in their lives in this materialistic world. Therefore, it may be said that one cannot reasonably find fault with the entire system of traditional Tantrism that includes *mantra, yantra* and *Tantra* on account of the prevalence of certain unauthorized rites and pseudo-*Tāntric* practitioners.

References

1. H.C. Das., *Tantricism - A Study of the Yōginī Cult,* Delhi, 1981, pp. 5-6.
2. S. Sankaranarayana., *Śri Chakra,* Pondichery, 1970 pp. 10-11.
3. N.N. Bhattacharya., *History of Tāntric Religion - An Historical, Ritualistic and Philosophical Study,* Delhi 1999, p. 346. The chief parts of the temples are viewed as in the form of a sexual design; the porch representing the lower end of the vagina up to the hymen, the hall or the vagina itself and the inner sanctum or the *garbha griha,* the uterus.
4. *Ibid.,* Also see *Śilparatnakōśa* edited and translated by Sthapaka Niranjan Mahapatra, pp. 3-7.
5. *Descriptive Catalogue of Sanskrit Manuscripts in the Collections of the Royal Asiatic Society of Bengal,* vol VIII, 6206, *Tantra Manuscripts,* Calcutta, 1940.
6. N.N. Bhattacharya., *op.cit.,* p. 346.
7. The foundation stone for the Śiva temple was laid along with *Kāmākhya pīṭha* in the year 1983 and subsequently on the discovery of *Śrī Chakra Mēru* in *pañcha lōha* form the *Śrī Chakra* temple was planned for its construction which was completed by 1990 (June) with the installation of the *Mūla Virāt* (Main icon) of goddess *Lalitā* who is also known as *Śrīdēvī,* or *Rājarājēśvari* or *Tripurā* Sundarī. The *guruji* of the temple gave her the name *Sahasrākshī.*
8. Balarama Srivatsava., *Iconography of Śakti: A Study based on Śrītattvanidhi,* Varanasi, 1978, pp. 118-124.
9. *Nityaṣōḍasikārṇava* VI, p. 24.
10. *Kāmakaḷāvilāsa,* XXXVI.
11. N.N. Bhattacharya., *op.cit.,* p. 440.
12. It is known as yab-yum in Tibetan.
13. *Sādhanamāla* II, p. 505.
14. Amritananda Natha., *Śrī Chakra Pūja.,* Devipuram, 2001, pp. 10-13.
15. The Tāntric texts have described different forms of *nyāsas;* See *Kulārṇava,* IV, p.18; *Śāradātilaka,* IV, pp.29-41; *Jāyākhya,* XI.
16. *Kulārṇava,* XVII, p. 54.
17. *Jñānārṇava,* XXIV, p. 54.
18. *Śrī Vidyā Nitya Pūjā Paddhati.,* Royal Asiatic Society of Bengal, vol. VIII, 6354, Calcutta, 1940. The other important works are

Śrī Vidyā Mantra Dīpika of Kasinatha and *Śrī Vidyā Ratna Sūtra*. For more details see Ch. Chakravarthy., *The Tantras-Studies on their Religion and Literature,* Calcutta, 1963, p. 75, 61 & 87.

19. K.K. Handiqui., *Yaśastilaka and Indian Culture,* Sholapur, 1968 p. 22.

20. *Siṁhāsana Dvātriṁśika* of Koravi Goparaju, vol. I, ch. IV v. 17, pp. 342-343.

21. Abbe Dubois., *Hindu Manners, Customs and Ceremonies,* Oxford, First edition 1897, pp. 646-648.

8

Fresh Light on Certain Obscure Tantric Practices in Daily Life

In the socio-religious and cultural life of the people of India the *Tantra* occupies a very important place with its vast literature embodying intricate ritualistic details. Through its literature the *Tantra* spreads the knowledge of profound things with the help of the mystic diagrams (*yantra)* and words or letters possessing esoteric meanings (*mantra*) to achieve the objective of the liberation of the soul. *Tantra* made a strong impact not only on the different religious systems but also on the social and cultural life of the people, and it became a part as well as a way of life of the people. The original purpose for which certain *tāntric* rites and rituals were performed during the earlier periods was completely forgotten and sometimes their original meanings and the implications are difficult to perceive. On the other hand, it is observed that the people, irrespective of their class or caste divisions and the religious faith they adhere to, follow such practices throughout the country with some modifications. In this chapter it is endeavored to throw some fresh light on certain customary practices that the people observe being unmindful of the original purpose and the *tantric* meanings embedded in them with the help of historical sources of the medieval times including inscriptional and literary evidences to project the profound impact of *tāntric* traditions in the daily life of the people.

Known by different names in different parts of the country—*alpana* in Bengal, *arpana* in Bihar, *rangōli* in Gujarat and Maharashtra, *kōlan* in Tamilnadu and *mṛuggus* in Andhra Pradesh—floor painting is a daily ritual and its observance is considered a good omen for the household. The practice of decoration of floors by using powders which is popularly known as *mṛuggulu peṭṭuṭa* in Andhra is an age old practice which is not entirely free from Tāntric influence and significance. Small designs are executed every day, while larger, more elaborate paintings are done on all ceremonial occasions. An important feature is that the entire pattern must be executed in an unbroken line, with no breaks anywhere for an evil spirit to enter. Although it is difficult to trace the origins and antiquity of this practice, it can be gathered with success from the historical evidences of the medieval times including the epigraphical and literary sources that it was quite a popular custom observed during the medieval times. Particularly the stone inscriptions found at Vishnu temples in Andhra at places such as Simhāchalam and Tirupati provide information with regard to this custom of adorning the floor of the temples for which some women were appointed for the purpose. However, the type of designs or the decorative motifs used in decorating the floors of the temples are not mentioned in them. On the other hand, literary sources throw a welcome light on this practice with regard to the nature of the practice, the method of application, the types of designs and other details. In *Kreeḍābhirāmam*, it is mentioned that the house of Māchaldēvī, a courtesan of Kākatīya king Pratāparudra, was decorated with *mṛuggus* in front of the house after sprinkling the water mixed with sandal-wood powder. In this context, it is stated that the *mṛuggus* were laid with *kāshmīramu,* which may mean to refer to saffron, which is red in colour and brought from Kashmir.[1] It thus shows that the *rangavallis* so described were further decorated with the application of colours. The materials commonly used for decorating the floors are lime powder and rice flour. By skillfully dropping the powder on the floor and by using the fingers the designs will be laid artistically. The decoration of the floors in front of the houses with *mṛuggus* has been mentioned in *Sukasaptati*.[2] It refers to the plastering of the floors with mud and its decoration by *mṛuggus (aliki mṛuggulu veṭṭinaṭṭi tinnelu)*. It is interesting to note from *Haṁsaviṁśati*, the several names of the *mṛuggus* that decorated the floors.[3] It describes how the ladies (*puṇya bhāminīs*) laid down different *mṛuggus* on the street roads on the occasion of the village festival (*tirunāḷḷu*) by using pearls, gems, topaz, emeralds, rubies and other precious stones. In this connection, it mentions the names of the designs laid on the floor as *kūrma, svastika, nabhōmanṭapa rangavallika, liṅga* with *svastika, srvatōbhadra, giribanda, mayūra nāṭya, nāga bandha, viñjāmara, vyajana, chatra, Siṁhatalata, brindāvana, kalpa vṛiksha, pāla samudra, gangā taranga, śankha, chakra* and *padma*. These references suggest that the designs for the *mṛuggus* are basically drawn from religious symbols and Hindu mythology besides indicating the continuity, in practice, of the art of ornamenting the floors. During the medieval period not only the individual householders decorated the floors of the houses but also the temples by the ladies appointed for the purpose. Inscriptions ranging between 13th and 15th century A.D. from Simhachalam reveal good information about this practice of ornamenting the floors of the temple of Lord Narasimhanatha. Generally the task of decorating the temple floors twice a day was entrusted to the *Sāni Samayamu,* a guild organization of ladies of the temple by the devotees who liberally made donations to the temple for the purpose of maintaining the service of *mṛuggulu peṭṭuṭa*.[4]

The *mṛuggus* drawn on the floors consist of several geometrical motifs, symbols and decorative designs. The set pattern of the *mṛuggus* laid on the floors in modern times reveal the inclusion of *nāga pāśa* design formed by the intricate coils of a serpent, intertwined serpents, *svastika,* the *aṣṭakōṇa* and *ṣaṭkōṇa* designs with *bindu* in the centre. The serpent is a symbol of life energy and is considered as the door-guardian. The use of *nāga* slabs in the temples is explained as serving the protective function from natural calamities. Symbols like *svastika,* lotus and *pūrṇa kalaśa* are considered as auspicious and would fulfil the cherished desires of the people. The *saṭkōṇa* symbol portrayed differently with angles around a central *bindu* or angles terminating with curvatures in the *mṛuggus* have meaningful depictions in *tāntric* art. It appears to be the *saṭkōṇa* of the *Anāhata chakra* of *tāntric* symbolism. Generally *yantras* consist of triangles cutting each other or straight lines crossing each other so as to produce a number of rectangular spaces and terminating in trident like projection. In *tāntrism, yantra* is a general term for instruments of worship. Worship of *yantras* and *chakras* that has been referred to in *Taittarīya Āraṇyaka* appears to be of ancient origin. It is observed that while performing any religious ritual, festival or worship of a specific God on certain occasion *mṛuggus* will be laid out on the floor after cleansing it with water. The *chakras* or *yantras* drawn with straight lines, triangles, circles and squares with lotus motif symbolize beauty, harmony and symmetry. Of several types of *yantras, Śrī yantras or Śrī Chakra* consisting of 43 triangles arranged in a lane is considered as the union of *Śakti* and *Śiva* while *Ṣaṭkōṇa yantra* is considered to be the symbol of creation of the Universe. During the medieval times the *Śākta* temples almost invariably contained the *yantras,* which forms the objects of regular worship. Probably in course of time, the *tantric* meanings, symbolism and significance of the *yantras* may have either got transformed or that the devotees lost sight of them and simply reduced them to a superstition. The common people used these *yantras* without realizing its philosophy and put them into common usage by regularly decorating the floors of the houses and temples with them, as they have believed that these mystic and magical diagrams would safeguard the interests of the people and ward off the evil from home and temples. Because of the *Tantric* origins, the practice of laying *mṛuggus* is still continued by the people without realizing their religious meaning and significance. The usage of *tāntric* diagrams and belief in the mystic potency of the interlacing triangles is not confined to the temples and houses of the Hindus alone, but extended to the monuments of the Mughal emperors also. It may be mentioned here that the monuments of Akbar at Agra and Fatehpur Sikri contain many Hindu art motifs like *Ṣaṭkōṇa, Svāstika, padma,* etc.[5] Of these *Ṣaṭkōna* is found on the tomb of Humayun at Delhi built during the reign of Akbar. These instances thus show that some of the geometric designs, particularly the *Tāntric* symbols, had attained mystic value and superstitious belief in the minds of the people, irrespective of their religious ideology that it would dispel the evil. From this it is evident that, although the knowledge of the original meaning and the symbolism of these *tāntric* diagrams was confined to the literate people of the society, the common people popularly used them to decorate the floors of their homes and temples since medieval times. It is found to be a practice that is observed till to date in many parts of the country with the strong belief that it would serve the functions of bringing auspiciousness, prosperity, protection from evils besides their aesthetic sense of beautification of their surroundings.

Mention has been made in *Dēvī Purāṇa* to the elaborate rituals observed while donating books to the temple or Brahmins. It states that the person gifting or donating the books should draw a *maṇḍala* with cowdung either in the East or North of his house in a quiet spot. Within this *maṇḍala* should be drawn a lotus with red colour which should then be decorated with flowers.[6] Here it is of interest to note that the drawing of designs on the floor and the specific mention of the use of red colour used for drawing the designs, are suggestive of the customary practice that was influenced by the Tantric religion.

In the *Tantric* religion the magical rites play a vital role. Magic is an illusory technique to control nature and is complementary to the deficiencies of real techniques.[7] The social significance of magic can be understood only against the background of the primitive undifferentiated collective life of the people. People in the ancient times believed in the supernatural powers of the *Siddhas*. In *Āpasthaṁbha* Dharma Sūtra and *Prapañchasāra* these powers by magical means were referred to as eight in number (*ashṭa siddhis*) that include *aṇima* (atomization), *laghima* (levitation), *mahima* (magnification), *garima* (greatness), *prāpti* (power of getting anything), *prakāmya* (non-obstruction of desire), *vasītva* (power of charming) and *īsvita* (sovereignty over all things).[8] The person who is endowed with these eight *siddhis* is considered a liberated soul. However, in the Buddhist *Tāntric* literature the list of eight *siddhis* is mentioned differently. According to *Sādhanamāla* it includes *khaḍga* (sword sanctified by spells for success in battle), *añjana* (collyrium that helps in seeing the concealed), *pādalēpa* (ointment applied to feet to enable one to move anywhere), *antardhāna* (to be invisible) *rasa rasāyana* (conversion of baser metal to gold), khēchara (to fly in the sky), *bhūchara* (going swiftly anywhere) and *pātāḷa siddhi* (diving underneath the earth).[9] The Telugu literature of the medieval times, particularly *Navanātha Charitra* of Gaurana contain the stories of nine *Siddhas* that revolve around the supernatural powers exhibited by them.[10] According to it, Meenanatha and his disciples during their wandering have tried out alchemy, *parakāya pravēśa* and at the attainment of *vajra dēha* besides exhibiting various powers of the *siddhas*. Likewise many romantic stories were woven out by the writers of the medieval times that reflect the contemporary socio-cultural life in Andhra around the use of magical staff, sandals and magical quilt of the *siddhas*.[11] The descriptive biographical accounts of the life stories of several Āndhra yōgis of the past two hundred years by B. Ramaraju based on the traditional accounts and oral traditions demonstrate the miraculous and supernatural powers of the saints such as *vasītva, sthaṁbhana* and their swift movement to distant places at their own will.[12] To cite a few examples it may be mentioned here of the supernatural powers of Lingāladinne Brahma Svāmi (1820-1890 with regard to his power of flying in the sky), Chirumalla Subbadāsu (1802-1882) who walked on the waters of the tank and Rama Svāmy (1700-1902) who was popularly known as Sorakāyala Svāmy who showed miracles like his knowledge of future events with accuracy, curing the people of diseases and liberating them from the possession of evil spirits. Many life stories of the *yōgis,* who led a simple life without aspiring for any material benefits reveal that the eight miraculous powers mentioned in the Tantra texts and secular literature of the period were not just imaginary ideas and that they have been practised successfully by the persons who attained those *siddhis*.

Besides the *ashṭasiddhis* there are six special rites in *Tāntrism* that have been characterized as black magic or occult practices. These rites are *māraṇa* (destruction), *uchāṭana* (driving away), *vasīkaraṇa* (bringing under control), *Sthaṁbhana* (arresting), *vidvēṣana* (causing antagonism) and *svastyāyana* (rites of welfare). The *Prapañchasāra* contains a *mantra* called *Tralōkyamōhana* for these six rites.[13] In the Vēdic literature also, one can find distinct references to the traces of *saṭkarmas* of the *Taṅtras* like *māraṇa, vasīkaraṇa,* etc. It is observed that some of the practices of witchcraft are almost identical with the similar practices mentioned in the *Tantras*. Besides the *Tāntric* works, even the secular literature of the medieval times also refers to the six magical rites which differ slightly from the list provided in the *Tāntric* works. Sōmadēva Sūri in his *Yaśastilaka* refers to them as *śānti* (cure of disease and expulsion of evil spirits such as *kṛityā), vasya* (bringing others under one's control), *sthaṁbhana* (paralyzing the activities of others), *vidvēshaṇa* (causing enmity between friends), *uchāṭana* (compelling one to abandon hearth and home) and *māraṇa* (killing).[14] Not only these *saṭkarmas* but also the 64 *siddhis* mentioned in the *Tāntric* texts include the major supernatural powers or *siddhis* that could be acquired through a variety of ritual practices. The great *Tāntric* mystic of 16th century informs us in his *Tārā Rahasyam* that the worship of *Tārā* or *Kālikā* leads to the attainment of various *siddhis* numbering 64 in all.[15] It is of interest to mention here that the list of the traditional 64 arts (*Chauṣaṣṭi kaḷās*) that dates back to the early centuries A.D. and has been revised by Vatsyayana had retained the traditional number 64 probably for the reasons that it was an auspicious number and that it has a bearing on the group of 64 *yoginis* of *Tāntric* religion. Further the great goddess herself is seen as an embodiment of the 64 arts and addressed as *Chauṣaṣṭi Kaḷāmayī* and is worshipped with 64 varieties of offerings.[16] The list of 64 *kaḷas* mentioned in the Telugu literature of the medieval times reveal that the list has been revised from time to time as one can find from the list furnished in *Siṁhāsana Dvātrimśika*[17] and *Haṁsaviṁsati.*[18] In these lists the magical rites including the *Ṣaṭkarmas* and other *siddhis* have been included. It is mentioned in *Siṁhāsana Dvātriṁsika* that the 64 *kaḷas* include *saṭkarmas,* which are described as *māntrikatvamu* (expertise in magic), *dūra gamanamu* (travel to distant places), *dūra śravaṇamu* (ability to hear from distance), *dhurandharatvamu* and *vasyākarṇamu.* Besides these, reference has been made to *jala sthaṁbhana, śilā sthaṁbhana, sthala sthaṁbhana, agni sthaṁbhana, khadga sthaṁbhana, vāyu sthaṁbhana, rasa staṁbhana, sukla sthaṁbhana, mahēndrajālamu, aṣṭavastu samuddharaṇa, adṛīsya karṇa* and *parakāya pravēśamu.* The long list of *kaḷās* mentioned above reveal that many of them were drawn from the *siddhis* and the 64 *kaḷas,* and that several *siddhis* were made accessible to the people as they were brought into the fold of the *kaḷas* to be learnt by the people.

The common Indian practice of burning the effigies of the enemies made out of straw (*kuśaputtalīka*), especially of the political and popular leaders of the modern times is nothing but the belief of the people in imitation of the magical rites.[19] It is observed that the enemies were destroyed or injured with the help of imitative magic. In this context may be mentioned the view of Frazer who says, "Perhaps the most familiar application of the principle that like produces like is an attempt which has been made by many people in many ages to injure or destroy an enemy by injuring or destroying an image of him."[20] The practices of *bāṇamati* and *chētabaḍi* that involve the making of an image with flour and other materials and piercing them with needles or causing injury to them by the *tāntric* practitioners by uttering some mystic *mantras* is intended to destroy the enemies. These practices are comparable to the *māraṇa*, one of the *ṣaṭkarmas* of *Tāntric* religion. In the historical literature of the medieval times also there are several references to the mystical and magical worship of the deities and the performance of the *tāntric* rites. In this connection, mention may be made here to the practice of offering the rice cooked with blood and bones to be offered to the spirits, *bhūtas* and deities to satisfy them and it is popularly referred to as *raṇaṁkuḍupu*. The deities invoked in this connection were *Mahākāḷi, Kālī,* Ḍākinī, *Vīrabhadra, Pōturāju,* etc.[21] Besides this to declare that the enemies were vanquished by the kings, the kings used to resort to the practice of making the effigies of their enemies and this practice is mentioned as *bomma peṭṭuṭa* in many literary works. Likewise, traces of the *ṣaṭkarmas* of the *tantras* like *māraṇa* and *vasīkaraṇa* can be found not only from the Telugu literary works of the medieval times but also from the observance of such practices even during the modern times.

The *tāntric* rites such as magic, charm and sorcery that form a significant part of the *tantra* system are observed in the modern times, as many of the *Tāntric* rites seem to have a universal character. For this reason, they became popular among the people distantly situated and having no cultural or ethnic affinity. The popular beliefs in the efficacy of *mantras, yantras* and *tantras* that involve the use of mystic syllables, diagrams and *mudras* the meanings of which are unintelligible and unknown seem to have become a way of life and sometimes it was by this means that attempts were made to acquire to control either one's own self or, if necessary, to get control over others. Perhaps it is because of this popularity of such *tantric* practices that the list of 64 *kaḷās* have incorporated in them the nine different aspects of arresting water, stone, place, fire, sword, air, emotions, semen and blood.

The wearing of protective amulets around the arms or waist by the children and others, a popular tradition that had its beginnings from the ancient times, must have been based on some *tāntric* practices. Studies conducted have revealed that irrespective of the religion, people believe in the mystic powers of the *taviz* given by the *sādhakas* or healers to safeguard themselves either from the evil spirits, enemies, ill-health or for their general well being. Recent studies conducted on the activities of the saints and sooth-sayers of the modern times throw a welcome light on the popularity and patronization of the *tāntric* practices, which could be a continuous popular cultural tradition.

Another interesting practice observed by several householders in the modern times is the practice of waving a lamp around the children or adults or animals by uttering some words to ward off the evil eye and is popularly referred to as *dṛishṭi*. Although the real meaning underlying this practice is not known, it seems to have had its beginnings from the ancient times. In his work *Yaśastilaka,* Sōmadēva Sūri mentioned it as the practice of *Nīrājana* offered to the horses at evening to dispel the evil eye. Sometimes, during the modern times red chillies are also used in such contexts, which are not referred to in any historical sources. On the other hand, it is observed that special significance is attached to the use of red colour in the rituals conducted for the deities. The option of red colour invariably for the garments to be worn by the *sādhakas,* the flowers offered to the deities and the increased usage of vermilion in the rituals offered to the *Śakti* goddess by the *tāntric* followers could possibly mean a substitute to the offering of blood to the divinity.

Thus the several cultural and customary practices observed by the common householders in their daily life during the modern times are not without any basis, reasoning and origins. But the real meanings of such practices were forgotten long ago and are found to be obscure to the modern mind. The study tries to bring to light the obscure *tāntric* meanings of certain practices like the ornamentation of floors, use of *chakras, yantras, mantras* and the wearing of amulets, etc. It also probes into the close affinities between the 64 arts of learning mentioned in the historical sources of medieval times and the 64 *siddhis* mentioned in the *tāntric* religion to highlight the impact of *tāntrism* on the socio-cultural life of the people.

References

1. *Kreeḍābhirāmamu* of Vinukonda Vallabharya ed. By V. Prabhakara Sastry., 3rd Revised ed., 1952, p. 58.
2. *Sukasaptati* of Palavekari Kadiripati, Hyderabad, 1979, canto III, v. 477.
3. *Haṁsaviṁśati* of Ayyalaraju Narayanamatya, Hyderabad, 1964, canot III, p. 140.
4. M. Krishna Kumari., *Facets of Andhra Culture,* Delhi, 1999. pp. 155-161.
5. R. Nath., "Depiction of a Tāntric Symbol in Mughal Architecture" *Journal of Indian Society of Oriental Art,* vol. VIII, 73-85.
6. Pratapaditya Pal., "The Gift of Books according to Dēvīpurāṇa" in M.S. Nagaraja Rao, ed. *Kusumāñjali-New Interpretations of Indian Art and Culture,* vol. I, Delhi, 1989.
7. N.N. Bhattacharya., *History of the Tāntric Religion,* 2nd ed. Revised, Delhi, 1999 p. 163.
8. *Ibid.*, p. 148.
9. N.N. Bhattacharya., *op.cit.*, p. 148-150.
10. *Navanātha Charitra* of Gaurana., ed. by K. Ramakrishnaiya., Madras, 1937, ch. III, IV & V.
11. M.S. Sarma., *History of Reddi Kingdoms.*, Visakhapatnam., 1948, p. 183, 100.
12. B. Ramaraju., *Āndhra Yōgulu,* (in Telugu), Hyderabad, 1998.
13. N.N. Bhattacharya, *op.cit.*, p. 148.

14. K.K. Handiqui, *Yaśastilaka and Indian Culture,* Sholapur, 1968, p. 406.
15. Saryu Prasad, ed., *Tārā Rahasyam* of Brahmananda Giri, Varanasi, 1970, p. 36-37.
16. R. Anantha Krishna Sastry., *Lalitāsahasranāma,* titles, 235, 236, p. 129.
17. *Simhāsana Dvātrimśika* of Koravi Goparaju, Kakinada 1933, canto 11, p. 113, lines 167-168.
18. *Hamsavimśati* of Ayyalaraju Narayanamatya., canto I, p. 37 line 155.
19. N.N. Bhattacharya, *op.cit,* p. 150.
20 Frazer, *Golden Bough,* London, 1900 vol I.
21. *Velugōṭivāri Vamśacharitra* v. 33.

Section - III
Art and Iconography

9

Pañchānana Gaṇēśa from British Museum: An Iconographical Study

In Hindu iconography the icons of *Brahma, Śiva, Agni* and *Vishṇu* generally show the multiple heads numbering three, two, four or five. But rarely, the images of *Gaṇēśa* who belongs to the family of lord Śiva are also shown with multiple heads. The extant images of *Gaṇēśa* reported from Varanasi reveal the manifestations of *Gaṇēśa* as *dvimukha, trimukha* and *pañchamukha*. Besides these, a few more images of *Gaṇēśa* having five elephant heads are reported from Orissa of which one is now exhibited in the British Museum, London. The *pañchānana Gaṇēśa* images, which are rare, pose complex problems in the history of art and Indian religious studies as regards to its origins and iconographical development. Further, in the appreciation of art and iconography of the images of *Gaṇēśa,* it is essental to focus on the strange physiognomical form of this god with five elephantine heads and an enormous belly, accompanied by the goddess and the mounts below them for the better understanding of the religious meaning and significance that the images symbolize. In the present chapter it is intended to highlight the composite nature of this deity and the diverse myths and religious motifs that came to be associated with his character in the Sanskrit texts including the *Purāṇas* that contributed to the iconography of *pañchānana Gaṇēśa* with special reference to the five-faced image of *Gaṇēśa* of the British Museum, that hails from Konark (Orissa).

Gaṇēśa with a single elephant head had been reported in early art forms as a garland bearer (or as *yaksha?*) in Amaravati railing sculptures (Madras Museum),[1] as *dvārapāla* at the entrance to the Buddhist caves at Bojjannakonda, A.P.[2] that had fallen under the influence of Mahāyāna Buddhism or as *dvārapāla* at Bhumra (of 5th century A.D.)[3] which was differently identified by Coomarasvamy as the *yaksha* form of *Gaṇēśa*.[4] Images of *Gaṇēśa* in different stances that is standing, seated and dancing or independently or associated with his consort as a cult god or as an attendant figure accompanying the figures of *Śiva* and *Pārvatī* and *Kārttikēya* or with the other *Gaṇas* are known through the stone-sculptures that spread over different parts of India. They reveal the development of the iconography of *Gaṇēśa* through the historical times. Interestingly, the images of *Gaṇēśa* have assumed multiple heads and hands, which carry different weapons and attributes for certain specific reasons. Usually, *Gaṇēśa* is invoked in the *dhyānas* as having one head, which, following the *Tantras,* should be one fifth of the total length of the body; but there are forms with two, three, four or five heads. It was observed by Alice Getty that *Gaṇēśa* with three heads was never represented in India and that the Hindus did not know him with four heads. But this is not true as P.K. Agrawal reports a few images of *Gaṇēśa* from Varanasi with multiple heads in the Indian context.[5] Besides these, a row of five elephant-headed figures seated in *lalita* posture close together in a row identified as *Pañch-Gaṇēśa* has also been brought to light from Varanasi. This unusual theme of *pancha Gaṇēśa* iconography has been corroborated by the further evidence of similar figures of *Gaṇēśa* known from Rajasthan through two sculptures.[6] Five standing figures including four *Gaṇapatis* in dancing postures and an elephant, all poised on lotus flowers, is noticed from a Śiva temple at Jamaroli near Jaipur. The mount of Gaṇēśa, a mouse, occurs below the figures in each case. Like the four human-bodied figures of *Gaṇapati* with elephant heads the freestanding elephant in the group also has a halo similar to that of the other figures and thus it represents the god *Gaṇapati* beyond any doubt. Another relief from the Somesvara temple at Kiradu depicts all the five *Gaṇapatis* in their usual elephant-faced human form.[7] Unlike the wall panel reported from Jamaroli the figures of *Gaṇēśa* are seated in a row representing an identical icon type, but with a difference in the attributes held by their hands and also the direction in the turning of their proboscis. The two figures on the left have their trunk turned to their right, a feature quite uncommon in *Gaṇapati* sculptures. From these two sculptures it is interesting to find the elephant without a human body along with the images of *Gaṇēśa*. Although there is no textual reference to the iconographic form of *Gaṇēśa* fully as an elephant, *Gaṇēśa* is referred to as *Gaja Vināyaka* in *Kāśī Khanḍa of Skanda Purāṇa.*[8] It has been described in the *Narasiṁha Purāṇa* that *Gaṇēśa* had assumed the form of an elephant to cause serious troubles to the demons.[9] In the *Gaṇēśa Purāṇa* of *Gaṇēśa Sahasranāma Gaṇapati* has been described as an elephant with its tail (*languḷa*) tying ropes or tying post (*alana)*, chains (*nigaḍa*) and a pond for merry-making (*kēḷī sarvōvara*).[10]

The icon of the five-faced *Gaṇēśa (pañchānana Gaṇēśa)* probably hailing from Konark (40" high) is now being exhibited in the British Museum (Pl. III). Thomas E. Donaldson described it as *Śakti Gaṇapati* since *Gaṇēśa* is shown as seated in *lalitāsana* holding a small female figure on his left thigh. He has ascribed the date of 13th century to the image under discussion.[11] The five-faced and ten-handed image of *Gaṇēśa* is highly interesting because of its iconography. The front right hand of *Gaṇēśa* is extended in *varada hasta* holding a pomegranate while his left hand holds a broken tusk. The remaining hands hold an *ankuśa,* arrow, trident and *chakra* while the corresponding left hands hold sugarcane, *nāga pāśa*, an ear of paddy and a lotus. The crescent moon adorns the *jaṭās* and the hair is arranged in *jaṭā mukuṭa*. The central forehead is decorated with dropping festoons of pearls falling from the headgear arranged as *kīrtimukha* at its base. While the central head is dominating that is depicted frontally, two heads on either side with the proboscis of each flanking face being curled up are carved. The trunk of the central head hangs straight down and it holds an indistinct object and curled to the right. The end of the trunk is curled and seems to balance a ball-shaped cake called a *mōdaka*. It is observed that in South India the proboscis practically is never shown lifting the cakes when turning to the right.[12] A trefoil shaped *tōraṇa* rimmed with beads frames the heads of the god. Behind the *tōraṇa* is found a tree with its branches spreading symmetrically to either side forming an ornate canopy with flowers and fruits being visible. Flying *vidyādharas* are carved on the two upper corners of the slab. Below the seated image of *Gaṇēśa* is found his vehicle rat beneath his right leg, while the elephant with its raised trunk is shown to the left side in smaller proportions. According to a South Indian legend, the presence of the rat, which usually accompanies *Gaṇēśa,* is connected to the absence of one of the tusks of *Gaṇēśa*. It mentions that once there was a giant demon with the face of an elephant that was unconquerable either by God or by man. Being a demi-god, *Gaṇēśa* fought with him with some possibility of success. During the course of his encounter with the giant demon, *Gajamukhēśvara* broke *Gaṇēśa's* right tusk, which was then caught by *Gaṇēśa* and threw it against the giant demon as a weapon. As a result of it the demon instantly turned into a rat and was taken into service by *Gaṇēśa* as his vehicle.

Usually *Gaṇēśa* is shown as a *brahmachārin* and is worshipped without his consort. But according to some legends he has two consorts called *Buddhi* and *Siddhi,* the personifications of wisdom and success. Although he is never shown in the accompaniment of these two consorts, he is carved along with a dēvī seated by his side or on his lap, and is referred to as *Lakshmī*. In the image of the British Museum, the goddess is shown as seated on his left lap with two hands in smaller proportions holding a lotus flower in her left hand by its long stalk, looking at the god in great adoration. The goddess is seated embracing *Gaṇēśa* with her right hand and she is decorated with *hāras,* armlets and bracelets. She wears *kirīṭa mukuṭa* on her head. The pedestal is decorated with stalks of foliage and on either side of the *asana* are shown the attendant figures, the mounts of *Gaṇēśa* and the goddess. The legs of the *asana* are decorated beautifully with a *gaṇa* supporting a *viraḷa* motif with a crouching elephant beneath the rampant lion. The carving of the female figure with *Gaṇēśa* is indicative of the influence of the *Tantras* and the popularity of *Śaktism*. The followers of the cult of Śakti Gaṇapati worship Gaṇēśa image in association with his female counterpart. The seated figure of *dēvī* on the left lap of *Gaṇēśa* is sometimes called *Lakshmī*. Gaṇēśa's association with other deities particularly with *Lakshmī* is known from a stone sculpture of 8th century A.D. now in the University Museum of Philadelphia.[13] In it *Gaṇēśa* is shown with a goddess on his right side. Interestingly it is a rare representation of *Svābhishēkamūrti of Lakshmī* as the goddess is shown receiving the *abhishēka,* possibly because of the round shaped symbols, which she holds above her head with her upper arms.[14] They may be taken for vases out of which water is pouring over her head. Generally *Lakshmī* is bathed with sacred water poured over her by two elephants from either side in the *Gajalakshmī* group. The presence of the elephants below the *Gaṇēśa* image along with his own mount clearly suggests that the goddess is no other than *Lakshmī*. *Lakshmī,* the consort of Vishṇu, is associated with elephants, rain and water and the religious myth of anointing the goddess at the time of the churning of the ocean of milk has been described in the *Mahabharata* and *Matsya Purāṇa*. Although there appears to be no direct association in the classical texts between *Lakshmī* and her elephant and *Gaṇēśa,* the connection has not been lost in the Hindu religion as both are bringers of well-being.[15] *Gaṇēśa* and *Lakshmī* are linked by the common figure of the elephant, as they are the deities whom the devotees venerate in seeking the fulfillment of their wishes and goals.

Gaṇēśa in the form of *Lakshmī Gaṇapati* or *Śakti Gaṇapati* was worshipped by the followers of the left-handed tradition (*vāmāchāra*) as the religious doctrines have admitted the inclusion of wine and women in their ceremonies.[16] Further the turning of the proboscis of the central (frontal) head of *Gaṇēśa* towards right instead of the left side is also suggestive of the *tantric* influence and rituals involved in the ritual tradition. In this aspect it is comparable to the group of five elephant-faced human forms of *Gaṇēśa* (datable to 11th century A.D.) of the Sōmēśvara temple at Kiradu, wherein two figures on the left, have their trunks turned to their right.[17]

The five-faced *Gaṇēśa* has been described in the iconographical texts like *Silparatna, Rūpamaṇḍana* and *Kriyākramadyōti* as *Hēraṁba Gaṇapati.*[18] Anantānandagiri's *Saṁkaravijaya* refers to a sub-sect of worshipprs of Ucchiṣṭa Gaṇapati who worship the deity called *Hēraṁba.*[19] The *Hēraṁba Upanishad* eulogises the five-headed form of *Gaṇapati*. This form of *Gaṇapati* is frequently represented in Indian, Nepalese and Tibetan art. In the art forms of *Hēraṁba* or *Pañchamukha Gaṇapati,* their heads are arranged in different ways; they bear different attributes, sit on different vehicles and are sometimes accompanied by a consort. In *Vidyārṇavatantra* there is no specific reference to the arrangement of the five heads. On the other hand it describes the colours of the five heads as white, yellow, dark blue, white and saffron.[20] The colours of the five faces of *Hēraṁba* show close similarity to those of the five aspects of Śiva, i.e., *Īśāna, Tatpurusha, Aghōra, Vāmadēva* and *Sadyōjāta. Śrītatvanidhi* describes the five faces as being the colour of pearls, yellow, dark blue, the colour of mother of pearl, and the colour of China rose (red). The similarity between the *dhyānas* of Sadāśiva and *Hēraṁba* is very much evident and has already been observed by art historians.[21] Although there is no textual description given for the arrangement of the five heads of *Hēraṁba,* dfferent art traditions are observed from the extant images. Broadly these can be categorized into four types based on the arrangement of the heads as mentioned below:

1. the heads are arranged in one row[22],
2. four heads are arranged on either side of the central head in two tiers-one above the other (in profile)[23],
3. four of the heads face the cardinal points and the fifth is put centrally on the top[24],
4. the heads are arranged in three tiers, all facing the front: three at the bottom, one in the second tier, and one in the third tier[25].

The image of *Gaṇēśa* from the British Museum is very much similar to the five elephant-faced *Ganesa* reported by Alice Getty found in the Munshiganj district, Dacca and an image of *Gaṇēśa* reported from the *Siddha Mahādēva* temple at Puri described below, as the five heads are in the same tier, that is, with two on either side of the central head which is much larger than the other four heads.[26] Likewise, the five-faced image of *Gaṇēśa* set up in a room over the image cell of *Dhuṇḍirāja Gaṇēśa* in the Visvanath Gali, Varanasi is also very much similar to the *Gaṇēśa* image of the British Museum in the arrangement of the five heads.[27]

The religious symbolism that lies behind the representation of *Pañchmukha Gaṇēśa* can be realized from the birth stories of *Gaṇēśa* contained in *Skanda Purāṇa*. According to one myth about the origins of *Gaṇēśa,* the elephant-headed demon Mālinī drinks *Pārvatī's* bath water mixed with her seed/dirt and produces a son with five elephant heads.[28] Śiva reduced these five faces to one thus amputating the four heads of *Gaṇēśa* in the process of cutting away *Gaṇēśa's* demon portion to render him fully divine. Thus the mythological story reveals the origin of *Gaṇēśa* from *Pārvatī,* who androgynously provides the creative substance and one demon mother Mālinī who brings forth the five-headed *Gaṇēśa.*[29]

An image of *Śakti Gaṇapati* (34"x20"), which is much closer to that of the icon of *Gaṇēśa* of the British Museum in its iconography has been noticed by T.E. Donaldson.[30] The image datable to 13th century is inserted into a niche flanking the entrance of *Siddha Mahādēva* temple at Puri. It has been assumed by Donaldson that originally it hails from Konark and kept in the niche at a later period. The five elephant-headed god is shown seated in *lalitāsana* with *Śakti* seated on his left thigh. The major right hand holds a pomegranate, while the left hand carries a bull *(ghanta)*. The remaining right hands hold a broken tusk, a small trident, an arrow and a *chakra,* while the corresponding left hands have a lotus, a small-stringed bow and a *gadā*. The proboscis is curled up to the left and holds an indistinct object. The head to the centre is shown in frontal position, while the other four heads—two on either side of the central one are depicted in profile. The hair has been arranged in a conical design ornamented with jeweled bands. *Sarpa yajñōpavīta* adorns the body and the lower garment is shown spreading on the *āsana*. The two-handed *Śakti* is shown seated in *lalitāsana* embracing the god with her right arm while she holds a lotus in her left hand. The lower part of the pedestal is missing and the vehicle of the god is not visible. Below the feet of *Gaṇēśa* is a large *ghaṭa* with stalks and leaves on either side. Excepting few variations in holding the weapons and the attributes shown in the hands, the rest of the iconographical features generally tally with those of the image of *Gaṇēśa* from the British Museum. Since the lower part of the pedestal of the Puri image is missing, the details of the mounts of the deities cannot be made out. The variations between these two images are in the manner of the curling up of the proboscis of the central head. While it turns to right in the case of the British Museum image, it is shown as curling towards the left side in the *Gaṇēśa* image of Puri. Further, the weapons like the small-stringed bow, *gadā* and bell are absent in the British Museum image, while they are present in the other image. Likewise it is observed that sugarcane, *nāga pāśa* and ears of paddy are present in the British Museum image that are absent in the image reported from Puri.

Thus it is observed that in the five-fold representation of *Gaṇēśa* there are different stages in the iconography of the god as it is evident from the extant images described from Varanasi, Rajasthan and Madhya Pradesh. In its first stage, the images of the four seated *Gaṇēśa* with elephant heads and an elephant form, the group of five gods and five lotuses along with the vehicle - rat-repeated five times near their feet indicate the divine status. And, in the next stage, five *Gaṇapatis* are shown in their common elephant-headed form. The iconographic study of five elephant-faced *Gaṇēśa* from the British Museum is quite interesting as it has revealed the worship of *Gaṇēśa* influenced by the *tantric* traditions giving rise to the creation of a new iconographic form such as the five elephant-headed god called *Hēraṁbā* in association with *Lakshmī* as his *Śakti* with the turn of the god's central proboscis to his right which is unusual, suggestive of the *vāmāchāra* traditions practised in worshipping the god.

References

1. Burgess, *Amarāvati,* pl. 30, No. 1.
2. D. Hanumantha Rao., "A Unique Sculpture of Gaṇapati from Sankaram" in *Śrī Rāmachandrika (Prof. Oruganti Ramachandraiya Festschrift) Essays on Indian Archaeology, History, Epigraphy, Numismatics, Art and Religion* ed. By A.V.N. Murty & I.K. Sarma, vol. II, Delhi, 1993, pp. 347-350.
3. Alice Getty., *Gaṇēśa*, Oxford, 1936, Pl. 3 (b).
4. *Ibid.,* p. 26; A.K. Coomarasvamy, *Yaksha* Pt I, Washington, 1928, pl. 23, fig 1.
5. *Dvimukha, trimukha* and five-faced *Ganesa* forms of late medieval period are reported from Varanasi by P.K. Agrawala; See, P.K. Agrawala., "Some Varanasi Images of Gaṇapati and Their Iconographic Problem" in *Artibus Asiae,* vol. XXXIX 1977/2, pp. 139-155.
6. R.C. Agrawala., "Newly Discovered Pañcha Gaṇēśa from Jaipur, Rajasthan" *Journal of Oriental Institue,* Baroda vol. XXI, Nos. 1-2, 197, p. 107, pls. I-II.

7. M.A. Dhaky., "Kiradu and the Maru Gūrjara Style of Temple Architecture" *Bulletin of American Academy of Benares,* vol. I, 1967, p. 42, fig. 68.
8. *Skanda Purāṇa, Kāsī Khanda,* 57, 104, p. 398.
9. *Narasiṁha Purāṇa,* 25, 13, p. 73.
10. *Gaṇēśa Purāṇa, Pūrvardha,* 46, 31-32, *Gaṇēśa Sahasram;* Also see, N.P. Joshi., "Purāṇas as Interpreters of Icons" in *Kala,* vol. VII, Delhi, 2001.
11. Thomas E. Donaldson., *Hindu Temple Art of Orissa,* vol. III, Leiden, 1987, p. 1244, fig. 2966.
12. Alice Getty., *op.cit.,* p. 16.
13. A. Coomarasvamy., *Yaksha,* Part II pl. 8, p. 73.
14. An image of Siva as *Svābhishēkamūrti* has been reported very recently. See S.N. Shivarudrasvamy., "Svābhishēkamūrti., A Rare Image of Śiva" in *Proceedings of Indian Art History Congress,* Delhi, 1999, pp. 81-83.
15. Paul B Courtright, *Gaṇēśa Lord of Obstacles, Lord of Beginning,* Oxford, 1985, p. 22.
16. Sir J. Woodroffe., *Shakti and Shakta,* p. 89.
17. M.A. Dhaky., *op.cit.*
18. T.A.G. Rao., *Elements of Hindu Iconography.* Vol. I Pt. II, Madras, 1914, Appendix - C, p. 7.
19. Anantanandagiri., *Saṁkaravijaya,* p. 87.
20. Gudrun Buhnemann., *Forms of Ganesa : A Study based on the Vidyārṇavatantra,* Wichtrach, 1989, pp. 66-69.
21. *Ibid.,* p. 66, foot note no. 2.
22. N. Bhattasali., *Iconography of Buddhist and Brahmanical Sculptures in the Dacca Museum,* Varanasi,, 1929, pl. LVIb; B. Bhattacharya., *The Indian Buddhist Iconography Mainly Based on the Sādhanamāla and other Cognate Tantric Texts of Rituals,* (Reprint) 1980, fig. 5; Balasubrahmanyam., *Early Chōla Art-* Pt. I Bombay, 1975, pl. 311; Alice Getty., *op.cit.,* p. 15, pl. 4 (b).
23. Prithvi K. Agarwal., *op.cit.,* fig. 18 (Varanasi image dt. 16th - 17th centuries A.D.)
24. T.A.G. Rao., *op.cit.,* vol. I, pl. XIII and XIV front and back view).
25. Alice Getty., *op.cit.,* pl. 19.
26. *Ibid.,* p. 15 pl. 4 (b); Thomas E. Donaldson., *op.cit.,* p. 1244, fig. 2967.

27. Prithvi K. Agarwala., *op.cit.*, p. 139-155.
28. H. Jacobi., "Brahmanism", *Encyclopaedia of Religion and Ethics,* 1914, pp. 807-808.
29. Paul B Courtright., *op.cit.,* p. 129.
30. Thomas E Donaldson., *op.cit.,* pp. 1244, fig. 2967.

10

An Image of Ādi Varāha in the Ashmolean Museum, Oxford

One of the favourite themes of the sculptors of Madhya Pradesh was the *Varāha* incarnation of lord *Vishnu* in both zoomorphic and anthropomorphic forms. The anthropomorphic forms of *Varāha* generally outnumber the zoomorphic forms and some of the zoomorphic forms are preserved in the museums of the State as well as in the museums abroad.[1] One such interesting *Ādivarāha* image is noticed in the Indian Art Collection[2] in the Ashmolean Museum at Oxford, U.K. (Pl.IV A & B) and is taken up for its iconographical study. Therein no specific details are given with regard to the place from where the stone relief sculpture was collected and it is mentioned vaguely as Northern Madhya Pradesh or Bihar and is dated to 9th-10th centuries A.D. Since the *Adivaraha* image carved in black marble stone is found to be highly interesting in view of the intricate carving on the body of the boar and the associated figures, an attempt is made here to analyse critically the iconography of the image for the better appreciation of its sculptural art and to understand the religious symbolism underlying the carving of this image. It is also intended to compare it with the images of this kind that are displayed, noticed and reported from Madhya Pradesh and Gujarat.

The image of *Ādivarāha* is approximately 3 ft. long and 4 ft high. It is shown as standing on the body of a full-fledged *kūrma* with raised neck. On its back is carved a seven-hooded *nāga*, standing with hands folded in *añjalī* pose. The image is carved as if it is on the verge of running. Near the raised right foot are carved the images of four-armed Brahma and Sāvitrī. Brahma holds *sruva* horizontally with his front two hands. The Vaishnavite emblems *śankha* and *chakra* are carved on the right side of the deity with the figure of *śankha purusha* in seated posture. To the left side of *Ādivarāha* is carved the standing image of Bhūdēvī, adorned with *hāras,* ornaments, long *vanamāla* and *karaṇḍa mukuṭa*. She is carved as two-handed and is touching the snout of *Ādivarāha* with her right hand for support, while her left hand is kept hanging to her left side. Between the front two legs is shown the *gada* and the *gadā dēvī* is seated to the left side of *Varāha*. The long tail of the *nāga* runs between the legs of *Varāha* and joins at the tail of it. The tails of the *sesha* and *Varāha* are knotted at the back of the *Varāha* and the *amṛitaghaṭa* is tied to them. The entire body of the boar is carved with the images of different divinities, sages, *airāvata, chandra, Kāmadhēnu* etc., in five rows on either side. It includes the divinities in standing and seated positions in rows. The standing images of the gods are noticed on the back leg to the right side and on two legs on the left side, most likely the images of *dikpālas*. Above the eyes and on the face of *Varaha* are carved divine beings such as the Sun, moon, planets and figures of goddess Lakshmi (?) or Gayatri (?). The neck of the *Varaha* is adorned with a garland with human figures. The face of the *Varaha* is carved exhibiting curved tusk and teeth. In the right and left ears the figures of a female and a male are shown seated in *lalitāsana,* respectively. It is observed that the figure on the right ear is two-armed and holds the sacred fire in them. She may be identified with the personification of *Iṣṭā* of *Dharma*. Similarly a two-handed male figure in seated position is carved in the left ear. But the details of the objects held in his hands are not very clear. This male figure may be the personification of *Pūrta*. In the *Vishṇu*

Purāṇa the ears of *Varāha* are compared with those of the *ishṭā* and *Pūrta* of Dharma, which are the feminine and masculine genders.[3] Probably for this reason the two figures in the ears of *Varaha* are carved differently as the female and male personifications of *Iṣṭā* and *Pūrta*.

An almost identical image of *Ādivarāha* has been reported from Vijapur, which is a *mūlabēra* in the·Rāmēśvara Mahādēv temple in Srimalivada in Vijapur.[4] The iconography of the image is entirely in agreement with the image noticed at the Ashmolean Museum. On stylistic grounds it has been dated to 13th-14th centuries A.D. Another image of *Ādivarāha* attributed to the same period is noticed at Vihar (Gujarat State), which is 14 kms fron Virajpur.[5] This image is stationed straight on the image of *Kurma* unlike the one found at Vijapur. The story of churning the milk ocean by devas and asuras was carved on the body of *Varāha*. *Śankhapurusha* and *Chakrapurusha* are shown seated between the right and left legs of *Ādivarāha*. The images of *dikpālas* on the top of the ears and the image of *Sēshasāyi* are carved on the head portion. The iconography of the image tallies generally with the *Ādivarāha* of the Ashmolean Museum. Besides these two images a good number of *Ādivarāha* images are in Modasa, Vihar, Unava, Mewad, Modhera and Valam in Gujarat datable to 10th and 14th centuries A.D. But these are somewhat different in their iconographical details from the image under study.

In Madhya Pradesh the zoomorphic forms of the *Varāha* are noticed at several places such as Eran, Khoh, Badoh, Mandasor, Hinglajgarh, Ujjain, Dudhai, Khajuraho, Udayagiri, Rajim, Samasgarh, Chandpur and Mandla. It is observed that the artists of Madhya Pradesh have excelled in demonstrating the concept of Supreme Soul and its creation in the image form.[6] In addition to the figures of the divinities on the body of *Yajna Varāha*, the *Varāha* is associated with the human figures personifying the *āyudhas* like *śankha, chakra* and *gada,* which are shown, seated to the right and left sides of the deity between the fore and hind legs.[7] In the images of the *Varāha* completely in zoomorhic form, the *Yajña* aspect of the *Varāha* is demonstrated in which each and every limb of the god is compared with each and every component of the sacrifice. To emphasise the concept of creation (*sṛiṣṭi)* the figures of divinities associated with the creation are carved on the body of the *Varāha*. In this process various elements of the sacrifice or yajña are compared to the various limbs of the boar in the *Vāyu Purāṇa*[8] and *Kūrma Purāṇa.*[9] According to *Sāttvata Saṁhita,* the body of *Yajña Varāha* holds the *Bhūh, Bhuvaḥ* and *Svāḥ* i.e., the creation of the Universe and the *Varāha* is considered as the Supreme God Vāsudēva.[10] The three *iṣṭis* of *Jyotiṣṭōma yajña* are compared to the neck of the *Varāha*, which is represented in the Khajuraho Varāha.[11] Likewise the two *iṣṭis* called *Prayanīya* and *Udayanīya* are compared to the tusks of the Varāha, which are personified in human forms and are represented in the *Varāha* images of the Central provinces of India. Similarly the two *dharmas* called *iṣṭa* and *pūrta* are compared to the ears of *Varaha* and are shown in human forms on the Varāha images except on the *Varāha* image of Eran. The sun and moon are compared to his eyes and the forehead to Brahma. The tongue of the *Varāha* is compared to *agni* and his hair to *darbha.*[12] In the sculptures of the later period goddess *Sarasvati* is shown in the form of having four arms, holding *Veena* in two hands and the other two hands with *varada* and *kalasa. Ananta Sēsha* or the Great Serpent is shown with the human form up to his waist level with serpent hood, on the tail of Varāha and between legs of the *Varāha* at the bottom. According to the *Śilpaśāstras, Varāha* should rest his right foot on the *kurma* shell. The zoomorphic forms of the *Varāha* in Madhya Pradesh are carved with the *Varāha* standing on the *kūrma* shell, resting his right foot on its shell with the raised head of the tortoise.

In understanding the iconography of the *Varāha* images the *Śilpa* text *Aparājitapṛichcha*[13] is very useful. In addition to that the texts like *Abhilashitārtha Chintāmani,*[14] *Chāturvarga*

Chintāmani,[15] *Rūpamaṇḍana,*[16] *Dēvatāmūrtiprakaraṇa,*[17] *Śilparatna,*[18] *Śilparatnakara,*[19] and *Mānasōllāsa*[20] contain valuable information with regard to the iconographical description. Besides these the *Matsya,*[21] *Agni,*[22] *Vishnudharmōttara*[23] and *Kūrma Purāṇa*[24] provide the iconographic canons of the *Varāha* incarnation of Vishnu.

The huge images of *Varāha* in their zoomorphic forms found at various places in Madhya Pradesh and Gujarat exhibiting the strength of virility are symbolic of the expression of the might and power of royalty. The image of *Varāha* in the Ashmolean Museum is not very much different from them in its iconography. The image under study exhibits the concept of Creation and *Yajña* on the body of the *Varāha* in the zoomorphic form by having the figures of various divinities. The carving of the images of *Sūrya* and *Chandra* above the eyes, the other divine beings on the body and legs in diminutive form, the careful execution of *kūrma* with raised neck in zoomorphic form, *sesha* in the combination of therimorphic form are indicative of the knowledge of the artist sculptors in the iconographic texts, Vēdic literature and the *Purānas*. The artist in such forms has emphasized the creation of Brahma on the body of the *Varāha* that includes *ekadasa Rudras, dvadasa Adityas, risis* etc. The representation of *Bhūdēvī* to his left side standing with two arms holding the snout of the *Ādivarāha* for support demonstrates the fact that the god has assumed this form for her sake only. Thus on stylistic grounds and on the basis of the associated figures i.e., the images of the *āyudha purushas* the *Ādivarāha* image under study can be ascribed to the period of 13th-14th centuries A.D. as it has some parallel images reported from Madhya Pradesh and Gujarat which are found to be similar in its iconography.

References

1. Haripriya Rangarajan., "Varaha Images in Madhya Pradesh: An Iconographic Study" Prof. K.D. Bajpai Memorial Lecture, in *Proceedings of the 8th Session of Indian Art History Congress*, ed. By C.P. Sinha, U.C. Dwivedi, Delhi, 1999, pp. 129-150. It

is reported that the total number of the images of Varaha in Madhya Pradesh are 86 out of which 29 are in zoomorphic form.

2. J.C. Harle and Andrew Topsfield., *Indian Art in Ashmolean Museum,* Oxford 1987.
3. *Vishnu Purana,* Book I Ch. IV, V. 34.
4. Haripriya Rangarajan., *Spread of Vaishnavism in Gujarat up to 1600 A.D.,* Delhi, 1990, fig. 99 and 100 p. 128.
5. *Ibid.,* fig. 101 and p. 129.
6. Haripriya Rangarajan., *Varaha Images in Madhya Pradesh : An Iconographical Study,* Mumbai, 1997, p. 183.
7. *Ibid.,* figs. 97, 99, 100, 105.
8. *Vāyu Purāṇa,* Vi v. 1-11.
9. *Kūrma Purāna,* Part I, VI, v. 1-25.
10. *Sāttvata Samhita,* XII, 46b-52a.
11. Haripriya Rangarajan., *op.cit.,* figs. 28,29,34
12. *Ibid.,* p. 36. Yajna Varaha is described in *Bhāgavata Purāṇa* (III, 13. 35-38), *Brahmāṇḍa, Prakriyapada* (5-9-23), *Brahma Purāṇa* (213, 33-37), *Harivaṁśa* (I, 41, 29-35 III, 34-41), the *Padma Purāṇa, Sṛiṣṭi Khanda* (16. 55-61), *Vishnudharmōttara Purāna* (I, 2-3-8) and *Vishṇusahasranāma* (v. 117).
13. *Aparājitaprichcha* of Bhuvanadeva, 25, v. 1-17, pp. 58ff.
14. *Abhilashitārtha Chintāmaṇi,* III, 1, 738-741.
15. *Chāturvarga Chintāmaṇi,* Dana Khanda, 327-328.
16. *Rūpamaṇḍana,* III, 24.
17. *Dēvatāmurtiprakaraṇa,* V 72-76.
18. *Śilpratna,* 25, 112-116.
19. *Śilparatnākara,* XI, v. 14.
20. *Mānasōllāsa,* Part I v. 699-702.
21. *Matsya Purāṇa,* 260, 28-30.
22. *Agni Purāṇa,* 49, 2-3.
23. *Vishnudharmōttara Purāṇa,* III, 79, 1-1.
24. *Kurma Purana,* Pt. I, VI, v. 1-25.

11

Some Aspects of Inscribed Jaina Images

Religions played a major role in the development of art, architecture and the craft works, particularly in moulding the metal images. Jainism contributed to the cultural heritage of the South to a great extent. The deep impressions that Jainism has left on the annals of Indian history and its contribution to the Indian thought and culture is considerable. One can gain this idea and trace the influence of the religion Jainism in the literature, arts and craft works of different periods of time. From the historical as well as the archaeological sources it can be gathered that the Jains have made remarkable contributions to the development of building arts, sculpture, icons and crafts works in metals.

Like the Hindu temples, the Jain *Basadis* were the centres of the five-fold activities of worship, feeding, medical care, shelter and education. It is quite often observed by the historians that the contribution of Jainism is not only unique but also substantial in terms of both quantity and quality. The art forms created by the artist - sculptors and the craftsmen of different regions of South India display a deep commitment to the Jaina *Dharma,* without sacrificing its inherent aesthetic appeal.[1] It is also widely felt that the Jain art and architecture of South India significantly reflects the philosophical and religious attitude as well as the cultural aspirations of the people. The development and growth of art and crafts depended largely on the ritual needs of the developing religious creed and its philosophy.

Jainism favoured the worship of the *tīrthāṅkaras* in image form that are enshrined in the Jain *Basadis* and in this aspect we do not find much difference between Jainism and Hinduism. As observed and rightly pointed out by Jyoti Prasad Jain as regards the spirit of Jaina art, the master artists not only adopted the architectural and sculptural styles prevalent in their places and time but also preferred to include contemporary cultural traits and ideology.[2] In the case of building the religious edifices in Jaina faith it is well noticed that the efforts went through more or less the same stages of development as those of the Brahmanical temples.[3] The Jain temples, since they catered to the social, economic and religious needs of the devotees like those of the Hindu temples, had to be quite large and beautiful enough to attract a large number of devotees and other people. On the other hand, it may be said that they had to foster the religious fervour of the people by the ritual worship of the icons. In image-making and image-worship Jainism took a lead and it is found that massive stone sculptures of Tīrthāṅkaras were consecrated in the sanctum-sanctorum of the Jain *Basadis*. Besides the main icons the *kautuka, utsava* and *abhishēka mūṛtis* or *bēras* in metal were also installed in the *Basadis* of which the majority of them were endowed with the characteristic features of *Jina*. In the present chapter, it is intended to study the inscribed images of the Jain Tīrthāṅkaras of South India in general and the two Jaina icons of 12th century A.D. preserved and exhibited in the Victoria & Albert Museum, London, in particular to offer plausible explanations with regard to the basic ideas and intentions of the artists, for carving the images in stone and metal with inscriptions as well as the value and significance of such inscribed images in the study of the history of religions.

From the *āyagapaṭṭas* found at Mathura, which are anterior to the Jaina images, we can get the earliest evidence of Jain worship. It is known from the inscriptions on the *āyagapaṭṭas* that these slabs were probably placed on the raised platform for worship.[4] The *āyagapaṭṭas* are of two types-having symbols and Tīrthāṅkara images with inscriptions. Many square stone slabs bearing mostly the figures of Jain Tīrthāṅkara in the centre and some auspicious motifs such as *svāstika, śrīvatsa, nandipāda, triratna, kalaśa, pushpadama, Vardhamāna, mīna, mithuna* and *vaijayanti*, etc., on its corners or sides have been found from Mathura that contained some inscriptions.[5] It is mentioned in some of the inscriptions found on these image slabs the purpose of setting up of *āyagapaṭṭa* as to the worship of the *ārhat* (*ārhat pūjaye*).[6] Another record on the *āyagapaṭṭa* having the relief of a *stūpa,* that belongs to the Kushāṇa times starts with salutation to *Ārhat* Vardhamāna and records the erection of a shrine of *ārhat (Ārhatō dēvikula)*, a hall of homage (*āyaga sabhā*), cistern (*prāpa*) and a stone slab (*śilā paṭo*) at the sanctuary of *Nirgrantha Ārhats (pratishṭhāpitō Nirgranthan Ārhatayatana)*.[7] The importance of the inscribed *āyagapaṭṭas* lies in providing an evidence of the transition in Jaina worship from symbol to icon and immediately followed by the production of a number of Jaina Tīrthāṅkara images.

The images of Tīrthāṅkaras are purely human in form. They do not exhibit any unusual number of heads, eyes, arms, legs, etc., like the Hindu Gods. Epigraphical references from 3rd century B.C. record the worship of Jina images. From the archaeological evidences it is known that the images were in demand from an early period and that certainly the worship of the Jaina images was well established in the Kushāṅa period (1st-3rd century A.D.). It appears from the epigraphs that the monks were encouraging the laity to commission images of the Jinas, to erect *basadis,* enshrine relics in them and visit the sacred places associated with the lives of the Jinas. Inscribed Jina sculptures from Mathura and Ahichchatra reveal this patronage. *Padmacharitra,* an early text of 473 A.D. extols the construction of the *Jina bhavanas* (image houses) and installing the images of Jina, although the Jain orthodoxy contradicted the image worship. *Padmapurāna* (7th century A.D.) also exhorts people to worship Jinas and erect the Jina images for the attainment of temporal as well as eternal blessings.[8] While carving the stone images or in making the metal images of the Jinas, the artists followed strictly iconographical and iconometric systems that prevailed during the contemporary times. By following the iconometric prescriptions laid down in the *śilpa* texts, they observed the measurements and proportions of the images and it is because of this observance of the iconometric conventions that the Jina images are found to display a remarkable degree of uniformity. It may be said, in this context, of the standardization of the meditating Jina figures, which are difficult to distinguish except by their identification through the cognizant mark that is usually depiçted on the base of the image. In spite of the fact that all the Jinas are of equal standing in Jainism, the images of certain Jinas seem to have gained greater popularity, as this is evident from the ratio of the extant images of different Jinas.[9] Of the images that have developed the cult practices mention may be made of Ādinātha or Rishabhanātha, Sāntinātha, Pārsvanātha and Vardhamāna, who deserve special mention besides the worship of the goddesses like Sarasvatī, Aṁbikā, and a few other *Śāsana dēvatās*.

In understanding the reasons behind the deliberate encouragement of the laity by the Jaina teachers for performing the image worship and also the erection of the Jina images, the inscribed images throw a welcome light. It is in this perspective the inscribed image of Ādinātha from the village Peravali of Karlapalem Mandal of Guntur district (now placed in Govt. Museum, Guntur) can be studied. The high pedestal of the standing image of Ādinatha contains an inscription— (*Ādināthasvāmy - Pratimāra - makattina - stāpita - Guṇa Nandi Ācharyana-*...) which states that a certain Guna Nandi Āchāri consecrated this Ādināthasvāmi image. Although the inscription is not dated, on the basis of its palaeographical characters, it can be ascribed to 4th - 5th centuries A.D.

Not only the inscribed Jina images provide the information about the cultic practices centered around certain Jina images, but sometimes they also brought to light evidence of unusual historical significance. Three inscribed tīrthaṅkara images were found near Vidisa, of which two of them are of Chandraprabha (8th Jina) and the third one is that of Pushpadanta (9th Jina) according to the inscriptions. While mentioning about the name of the Jinas that were consecrated, information is also given about the donor of the images. In this connection, the three inscriptions of the Jina images refer to *Mahārājādhirāja* Rāmagupta as responsible for the carving of these images.[11] K.D. Bajpai has identified Ramagupta with the elder brother of Chandragupta Vikramaditya and the Gupta ruler known from his copper coins in large number from the Vidisa region, who bore the title of *Mahārājādhirāja* like the other rulers of the Imperial Gupta dynasty. The label inscriptions on the Jina images thus provide some valuable information of the installation of the Jina images by the Imperial Gupta rulers, whose historicity and identification posed problems and remained as a controversial issue till the discovery of the inscribed Jina images. Further, it reveals the continuation of the practice of the carving and worshipping of the Jina images during the Gupta period.

The inscribed images of Jinas on the hill at Konakondla closely resemble the Jina images reported from Pedatumbulam (No. 2505 of the Madras Museum) and the two images from Vemulavada in their execution and the iconographical details.[12] The Konakondla images carved on red slab stone are about four and a half feet high and have circular *prabhas* round their heads and stands on a lotus. The triple parasol is found above their heads and the images are in *kayotsarga* posture. Another interesting thing is that a sketch of a Jina in *kayotsarga* posture is incised on the hill on horizontal level and rocky ground suggesting the idea of the sanctum of an open Jinalaya to be constructed on the hill. Although S. Gopala Krishna Murthy has stated that the writing below the Jina figures was a Rashtrakuta habit,[13] it is difficult to agree with him as the archaeological evidences present a different picture. Another important Jaina centre that gave rise to the inscribed Jina images is Danavulapadu (Jamalamadugu Tq of Cuddapah District). From the inscription of the Jina image it can be gathered that the Rashtrakuta king with the title "Nityavarsha" (Indra III or Govinda III ?) was responsible for the installation of the Jina image.[14] Another image inscription mentions the construction of a stone seat for the bath of the image of Śantinātha by the same Rashtrakuta king who is referred to by his title only.[15] These records provide ample evidence for the royal patronage extended by the Rakshatrakutas for the worship of the Jina images.

The image inscription found on the pedestal of a Jina image in the Rajesvara temple of Vemulavada (Siricilla Tof. Karimnagar District) refers to the construction of a Jain temple named *Subhadāma Jinālaya* by Baddega for the favour of a scholar Sōmadēva Sūri of the *Gauḍa Saṅgha*.[16] The temple referred to in the inscription can be identified with the *Subhadāma Jinālaya* of Vemulavada and the Sōmadēva Sūri with the author of *Yaśastilaka Chaṁpū*. The image of Pārśvanātha and another Jina image housed in the Hyderabad State Museum, containing the inscriptions on the pedestals informs us that the images were installed and the *māṇḍalika* chiefs constructed the temples for them. The insertion of the Jina images into the walls of the Hindu temples and worshipping them as a god along with the other Hindu divinities can also be noticed from Andhra region (Pl.V C&D). One label inscription on a Jina image in the characters of 8th century A.D. has been noticed at Kesanapalle (Gurazala Tq. Guntur District) with the word *chalēśvara*.[17]

Although the figure label inscriptions are short and sometimes fragmentary in nature, rarely they provide the details of the name of the sculptor also. The best example is the inscribed image of the 23rd Tithankara - Parsvanatha-carved in black shale stone that hails from Gulbarga, Karnataka State, and this image is now exhibited in the Victoria and Albert Museum, London (Pl. V A). The Jina is carved as standing in *kayotsarga,* setting himself free of the body from all the earthly distractions. Above his head the *Nāga* is shown as protecting him, while the figures of *Yaksha*, *Dharanendra* and *Yakshi Padmāvathi*, are carved on either side. The coils of the serpent can be seen at the back of the image. The hair is done in the shape of ringlets. The figure is nude and the face is serene. The seven-hooded serpent is shown prominently over the head of the Jina. Above his head is carved the three-tiered parasol. His hands reach up to the knees. The figure is highly polished. The inscription below the pedestal in the Telugu Kannada script of 12th century A.D. refers to the carving of the image after a period of persecution and that the image was made for a temple after its restoration. It also mentions the name of the sculptor as Chakravarti Pālōja and such type of reference to the sculptor is a rare occurrence. Although this image is comparable with the Pārśvanātha images reported from Hyderabad State Museum[18] in its iconography and iconometry, the image under consideration is important since it provides the information about the sculptor and also of the restoration of a Jain temple after the period of persecution.

Inscriptions on the pedestals or below the Jina images are found not only on the stone sculptures but also on the metal images. From the religious and artistic point of view the Jaina metal images are highly important. The inscriptions found on the metal images help us in dating the imges, and in tracing the various stages which metal art underwent in different periods. Sometimes they provide the crucial and important information like the triumph of the Jina over the other gods or religious faiths. The inscribed bronze image of Śāntinātha in seated posture displayed at the Victoria and Albert Museum, London (Pl. V B), is a rare example of bronze casting that bears an inscription dedicating to the triumph of Śāntinātha in Vikrama year 1224 (A.D. 1168). This remarkable-large-scale, solid-cast image depicts the 16th Jina enthroned on a jewelled cushion and surrounded by celestial attendants, elephants and musicians. He sits in a *yogic* meditation posture, with his hands gently resting, one on the other. Śantinātha was a very much—venerated god both by the monks and the laity as the preserver of Jainism at a time when it was in danger of extinction.

Thus the study of the inscribed images of the Jinas has brought to light certain important issues like the idol worship in Jainism, the transitional stage of worshipping the sacred symbols and Jinas with the help of *āyaga-paṭṭas,* the dating of the images on the basis of the label inscriptions, which are either dated or undated and the construction of temples for enshrining the images or indicating the practice of open *jinālayas* on hill tops or in natural cave shelters. These image inscriptions have also provided the useful information with regard to the identification of the dynastic rulers whose historicity is questionable. The royal patronage extended to the writers and poets of the Chalukyan period by way of installation of Jina images and the construction of the Jain temples for the merit of the donee is evident from the image inscriptions. Further the study brings to light the names of the sculptors who were responsible for carving the images, the restoration of the Jain temples after the period of crisis marked by religious persecutions and the dedication to the triumph of Sāntinātha in the 12th century A.D. on the basis of the inscribed Jina images reported from Karnataka and Western India and now exhibited in the Victoria and Albert Museum.

References

1. Raghunath Bhatt., "Jain Contribution to Art and Architecture" in Haripriya Rangarajan et al. ed. *Jainism Art, Architecture, Literature and Philosophy,* Delhi, 2001, p. 216.
2. Jain Jyoti Prasad., "The Genesis and Spirit of Jaina Art" in A. Ghosh ed., *Jaina Art and Architecture* vol. II, New Delhi, 1975, pp. 35-40.

3. K.V. Sounder Rajan., "Monuments and Sculpture A.D. 1000 to 1300: the Deccan and South India" in A. Ghosh ed., *op.cit.,* 1975, pp. 310-334.
4. R.C. Sharma., *Mathura Museum and Art,* Mathura 2nd ed., Delhi, 1976, p. 36.
5. V.S. Agrawala., "Catalogue of Mathura Museum", *J.U.P.H.S,* XXIII 1950, Pts. 1-2, pp. 69-7; Antiquities Nos. Q2, 569, 1603, 2313, 2563; A. Ghosh., *op.cit.,* Pls. 1, Mathura Museum, Q2, 2B, SML (J255), 14 (SMLJ 250), 15 (MMS, 49), 16 (SMLJ 248).
6. D.C. Sircar., *Select Inscriptions,* Calcutta 1942 Bk. II No. 25, pp 118-119.
7. A.L. Srivastava., "Mathura: The Cradle of Indian Cult Images" in Devendra Handa, ed. *Indological Studies* (*Essays in Memory of Shri S.P. Singhal*), Delhi, 1987, p. 55.
8. *Padmapurana* Pt. I, ch. 14, vv. 92-93, p. 313; also see Ram Bhushan Prasad Singh., *Jainism in Early Medieval Karnataka,* Delhi, 1975, p. 24.
9. P. Pal (Ed)., *The Peaceful Liberators: Jain Art from India,* Thames & Hudson, London.
10. G. Jawaharlal., "Adinatha Worship in Andhra" in *Proceedings of Andhra Pradesh History Congress,* XXVIth Session, 2002, Anaparti, p. 40.
11. K.D. Bajpai., "Ancient Jaina Art of Madhya Pradesh" in R.C.Dwivedi, ed., *Contribution of Jainism to Indian Culture,* Patna, 1975, pp. 196-199.
12. S.Gopala Krishna Murthy., *Jain Vestiges in Andhra,* Hyderabad, 1963, p. 30-31.
13. *Ibid.*, p. 31
14. G. Jawaharlal., *Jainism in Andhra,* Hyderabad, 198, p. 190, No. 18 - Danavulapadu Inscription.
15. *S.II. IX,* pt. I No. 63; 83 of *Inscriptions of A.P. Cuddapah District,* vol. i, p. 92.
16. *Ibid.*, No. 20; p. 194-195.
17. *Ibid., APGRE* of 1965, No. 93.
18. Kiran Kranth Choudhary., "Some Parsvanatha Images from Telangana" in Haripriya Rangarajan et al. *op.cit.*, p. 158-160.

SECTION - IV
ROYALTY, WOMEN AND SOCIETY

12

'Divine Kings' and the Concept of Kingship in Medieval South India

The ancient texts on statecraft and polity have shown kingship mainly from the religious point of view. In ancient times no distinction seems to have been made between religion and state government as everything was viewed through the lenses of religion. The scriptures of all religions have prescribed and taught nearly identical ethics. Everywhere in the world, generally the people be it the Hindus in India or the Muslims in the Islamic countries or the Buddhists in Japan—have regarded their ruler as the Divine being on earth and his rule has been accepted as having divine sanction.[1] It is interesting to mention here that the earliest Japanese word for government is *matsuri-goto,* meaning religious observance or worship.[2] It demonstrates the identity of religion and politics and also is suggestive of the lack of differentiation of function between the two different spheres. Further it may be noted here of the reference to the king in ancient Egypt as Pharaoh meaning the earthly representative of God. To strengthen this line of argument, the usage of the two terms from the Indian perspective—may be cited 1) *Dharmaśāstra*—for a code of laws and 2) *Nītiśāstra*—for polity occurring in the ancient Hindu scriptures. The words *dharma* with its meanings—religion, duty, law and *Nīti* with its meanings—ethics, polity, etc., have proved flexible enough for a variety of interpretations to suit the changing needs of the people from time to time. In Hinduism, the king plays a central role by guaranteeing the overarching moral order of society and the cosmos-the *dharma* in a holistic sense. The king is the earthly agent of the deities and sponsors their worship, like the lordly patron (*yājamana*) of the Vedic sacrifice. The king was supreme in his court as the gods in the temples under his protection.[3] The historians and the indologists have shown that the king was the divine being as he is represented as the fifth *lōkapāla* (guardian deity) in the literature and inscriptions.[4] In the copper plate inscriptions of the Pallavas of 5th and 6th centuries A.D. the Pallava kings are referred to as *pañchama lōkapāla* with the view that he is the protector of the central region of the earth while the other four guardian deities are in charge of the four quarters of the universe. Similarly, in the Buddhist literatures also the *lōkapālas* are referred to as *mahārājas*, a term used to refer to the ruler of a territory. This suggests that the kings were attributed with divinity and it was well accepted by the elite of the ancient Indian society. Burton Stein has stated that the Indian kings, though not gods themselves, like the kings of southeast Asia were conquerors, successful warriors, capable of inspiring lesser chiefs and kings to ally for plunder and glory as for territory. He also expressed that the royal authority depended on persuading lesser authorities—chiefly heads of peasant institutions—to accept their offers of protection in return for a portion of their subjects' wealth.[5] In the Integration Model of state formation in early medieval India, Hermann Kulke has suggested the chronological dimension in three sucessive stages of state formation called chiefdom, early kingdom and imperial kingdom. This corresponds with the evolution from king (*rāja*) to great king (*mahārāja*) and supreme king of great kings (*mahārājādhirāja*). A continuous and multifarious process of state formation is suggested rather than static structural features of the state and its society.[6] Along with these changes, the concept of kingship and the functions as well as the duties of the king have taken a new turn and dimension during the medieval times. This could be perceived in terms of the relation between the king and the people. Contrary to the concept of 'divine king', who was not hesitant to exploit the people to collect the State revenues or to win the enemies by espousing the superstitious beliefs and publicizing them, as explained by R.S. Sharma[7] on the basis of Kauṭilya's *Arthaśāstra,* the medieval kingship was viewed differently by the elite of the society. While accepting the divinity of the kings, people preferred to designate him as the lord of the earth and people. In the present chapter it is endeavoured to probe into the changes in the concept of kingship and the attitude of the people toward the king and his relations with the people of the society. For this purpose, the 'Kauṭilyan King' who is otherwise symbolized as the "Divine King" has been compared with the medieval king wherein the king was treated as the ruler of the land and people and who is committed to the welfare of the people. For this purpose literary works like *Rukmāngada Charitra* and *Āmuktamālyada* are taken as the major historical sources besides some inscriptions.

In his work on polity, Kauṭilya had explicitly demonstrated the practical character of the statecraft in which his lack of faith in the efficiency of certain religious practices and exploitation of the credulous beliefs of the people for the promotion of the interests of the State are revealed.[8] To augment and promote the royal treasury several superstitious devices were suggested by Kauṭilya to be followed by the king.[9] The king was more often associated with divinity and in order to impress the people with his super human powers and to infuse enthusiastic spirit among his own men and frighten his enemy's people, the king might undertake certain magical performances. To declare his association with gods, the kings resort to hold conversation with his spies, who suddenly emerge as fire gods amidst the fire and hold conversation with women of Varuṇa or of Nāga when they are performing magical tricks in water. All this was intended to publicize so that all the people in the country would know about the wonderful performance of the king and his association with the Gods. For this purpose the services of astrologers, soothsayers, horologists, story-tellers (*paurāṇikas*), spies and disciples are to be utilized. In the foreign countries also they should spread the news of gods appearing before the king and of his having received from heaven weapons and treasure, the two important elements of the State. In this connection, it is also mentioned that they should make it known to the people of the enemy that the conqueror is capable of interpreting dreams and following the language of beasts and birds and hence the victory is assured to the king. It is explained that the several devices and tricks played by the kings and his men were all a part of the skillful propaganda to convince and impress the masses of the divine character of the king with the view to gain the support of the people whole heartedly in the several aggressive designs planned against his enemies and those of the enemy might transfer their allegiance to the new conqueror. Thus a number of superstitious practices proposed by Kauṭilya in his work are stated to be the deliberate attempts to over-awe the masses into allegiance to the State. The politics expanded in *Arthaśāstra* had resulted in depriving the people of their earnings and in mobilizing them for furthering the aggressive designs of the conqueror as well as for destroying the enemy of the king. Sowing the seeds of illusion in the masses about the supernatural powers of the ruler was the main objective and function of the propaganda machinery advocated by Kauṭilya. Because of the ceaseless and effective propaganda, even falsehood also appeared as truth ultimately. Kauṭilya's attitude on the issue can be stated, as what is superstition for the ruler is true faith for the masses as sometimes the king conveniently escapes, evades or violates the performance of certain sacrifices to gods on certain occasions. Not only the work *Arthaśāstra* that refers to some superstitions but even *Agnipurāṇa* also mentions witchcraft, black magic and superstitions included in the religious beliefs. It gives several incantations (*mantrās*) that can ward off evil, remove desires and even kill one's enemies.[10] Incantation for obtaining victory in the three worlds and bringing about the death of one's own enemy are described in *Agnipurāna.*[11]

The ideology of Hindu kingship has been changed during the medieval times and the kings of large kingdoms rose to the status of earthly representatives of the tutelary deity, generally Śiva and since 12th century it is Viṣṇu. Even the position of the Gods has also been elevated and they were referred to as *Devadeva* and *Mahadeva.* The development of Hindu temple architecture both in its elevation and ground plan reflects the new royal ideology. In a way, the temple rituals are so evolved to assimilate the palace rituals. By constructing lofty temples the State religion has been developed. The systematic enlargement and embellishment of already existing holy places can be seen besides the development of the temple towns and cities. The political significance of the temple towns lies in the fact that they played the role of cosmic centres and the source of the highest legitimation of the royal authority.[12] In some cases the founders of the temples were included in the mythological legends and *sthalapurāṇas* of the temples in which they were treated as the mythical heroes of the past. The best example is the *sthalapurana* of Puri temple that refers to the construction of Jagannath temple by king Indradyumna by which the famines and mass deaths came to an end in Orissa and as a result the people had happily submitted to his rule.[13] Thus it is quite convincingly argued through the theory of integration that the temples of the medieval times as sacred centres are instrumental in the legitimization and the sanction of political power and that they provide ritual means for status confirmation as well as elevation and function as public arenas in which symbolic actions ratify existing systems of clientship and loyalty. In the inscriptions of the Eastern Gangas the king is described as the personification of God. This can be gathered from the terms attributed to the Ganga king Anantavarma Chōḍadēva who is referred to as *Trikaliṅgadēva, Kaliṅgēśvara, Ganga Nārāyaṇa, Ganga Mārttāṇḍa* and *Dēvādēva.*[14] Some of these terms reveal that people had great regard for their king as they have gone to the extent of personifying the king as God and considered him as the incarnation of Śiva and Viṣṇu. This kind of references in the inscriptions is not entirely new as the inscriptions in Andhra mention the rulers as *Paramēśvara, Paramamāhēśvara, Rājā Paramēśvara.*[15] Particularly, the Vijayanagara rulers were invariably referred to as *Rājaparamēśvara* in their inscriptions. In the case of the Chōḷas, the cult of *Dēvarāja,* i. e., the practice of worshipping the idols sometimes called after the living monarchs or after their demise is attested by the inscriptions.[16] This practice of deification of the king and construction of temples either in the name of the deceased or living king was quite popular in the Tamil region. The best examples are Ādityēśvara temple at Tondamanad built by Parantaka I and Arinjigai Īśvara temple at Melpāḍi built by Rājarāja I.[17] The naming of the gods of the temples after the chief patrons was also quite popular in Andhra during the time of the rule of the Chāḷukya-Chōḷas and the Kākatīyas. The names of the Gods like *Paṇḍēśvara, Chōḍēśvara, Bētēśvara, Gaṇapēśvara, Bhīmēśvara, Kētēśvara* are some examples in this context. Thus during the medieval times, the king was personified as god and attributed with divinity; as a result the temples became the sacred centres of power and authority besides being the political centres or the capital cities of the State. Heesterman has rightly pointed out that the sacred centres remain inherently associated with dynamic movements exercising its pull over long distances. It became the ritual space in whch human was integrated with divine activity.[18] Through the devotional faith that was well propagated which centered on God in the temples and with which, the kings were personified, the kings could control the people and the territory. Further it is also evident that the kingship has been developed in South India in which he could perceive how the religious imagination had increasingly encroached upon political ideology, resulting on one hand in a royal court emulating the court of God to the point of absurdity and on the other hand in sacred centres from political stability and cohesion emanate. From the available historical sources analysed above it is apparent that the temples are instrumental in the legitimizing of kingship and the sanction of political power to the kings.

The Telugu literary work *Rukmangada Charitra* written by Mallana (14th c. A.D.) refers to the functions, duties and responsibilities of an ideal king. In this context, it is to be noted that the terms mentioned with reference to the king are not divine and on the other hand they refer to his communion with the people and the land.[19] The different terms used in the work while referring to the king are given below to show how differently the king has been looked upon from the earlier concept of the divine king.

1. *Avanīpati*
2. *Jagatīpati*
3. *Bhūpati*
4. *Bhūbhujuḍu*
5. *Bhūmipālakuḍu*
6. *Bhūmīśvaruḍu*
7. *Bhūvallabhuḍu*
8. *Dharaṇipāluḍu*
9. *Dharaṇīpati*
10. *Kshitināthuḍu*
11. *Mahīpāluḍu*
12. *Prajāpati*
13. *Naranāyakuḍu*
14. *Mānavapati*
15. *Jananāyakuḍu*
16. *Janapati*
17. *Naranāthuḍu*

The above terms clearly suggest that the ideal king has been viewed as the head or lord of the people in this mundane world and that the relationship between the king and the people was guided by *dharma* and *nīti* as laid down in the *Śāstras*. Unlike the Kauṭilyan king who was sanctioned to collect the extra dues, levies or taxes from the people by exploiting the people through spreading the superstitious beliefs about the king as having embodied the supernatural and divine powers, the king described in *Rukmāngada Charitra* was warned against the collection of excessive taxes. The collection of unjust and excessive taxes was compared to the practice of fleecing the cow dry and leaving the calf without milk.[20] The collection of money from the people with the plea of the need was compared to the digging up of tanks in large numbers to catch the fish to eat.[21] It is further mentioned that it is the duty of the king to provide different kinds of seeds required by the people and the peasants for the promotion of agriculture in the country.[22] The king was advised to collect the revenue from the people cleverly like a butterfuly.[23] It emphasized the morality to be observed by the king as well as the people of the state towards the preservation of the law of the kingdom. In *Āmuktamālyada* also king Yamuna explained to his son the principles of statecraft before he retires to the woods. While cautioning the king against the officers whose acts are detrimental to the people, state and society, it is mentioned that the ideal king should get rid of those of his officers "who act like a jackal on the battle field, fail to persuade the poverty-stricken peasants from migrating and sell away their grain, cattle and timber.[24] With such officers none can prosper though one may conquer the seven worlds. All these references suggest the change in the outlook of the elite of the society, which reflected in suggesting various means and methods to be adopted by the ideal king towards building a welfare State and Society. Not only the kings but also the people were also very much concerned about the welfare and the glory of the king. Several inscriptions issued by the common people can attest this. The nobles and officials gave the donations and endowments for the religious merit, welfare and the prosperity of the kings.[25]

Thus it can be seen from the historical sources how the outlook of the people towards kingship has been changed from the king embodied with divine rights to that of the kings committed to the service of the people and the kingdom. The literary texts of the medieval times have explicitly mentioned that the ideal king should not be oppressive, should earn the goodwill of his subjects, ensure the prosperity of his people, impose light taxes, provide facilities for agriculture, detect crimes, safeguard the interests of the people, protect them from the attacks of thieves, punish the criminals, erring officers and maintain law and order.[26] Although the kings of the medieval times were also treated as the divine kings like the earlier periods, the divine right of the kings gave place to the principle of service to the people. In practice also we can notice from the records how the punishments were imposed and works of public utilities such as water tanks and reservoirs were constructed with the initiative of the king. The sacred centres patronized by the king and the state also provided various services to the people in times of national calamities and requirements of the people. Thus in spite of the fact that the medieval Hindu kingship was embedded spiritually in a network of relations with the sacred centres (holy places) of divine manifestations the medieval kings were mostly committed to the welfare of the people and society. There may be gaps between what is prescribed in the literary works as the duties and functions of an ideal king and what was actually pratised, but we cannot ignore the writings of Mallana and Krishnadevaraya, as Krishnadevaraya himself was the king of the Vijayanagara period who was highly committed to the service and welfare of his subjects.

References

1. *Manu Smriti,* Vii-4ff; *Vishnu Purana*, I. 13ff; *Brhaddharma Purana,* III, 37.
2. Sanson., *Japan: A Short Cultural History,* 51; R.N. Bellah., *Tokugawa Religion,* Illinois, 1957, p. 87; M.G. Panse., "Religion and Politics in Early Medieval Deccan A.D. 1000-1350 in

Religion and Politics in Medieval South India, Papers of a Seminar held by Institute of Asian Studies and Andhra University, 1972.

3. C.J. Fuller., *The Camphor Flame - Popular Hinduism and Society in India,* Delhi, 1992, p. 19; Louis Dumont., *Homo Hierarchicus: The Caste System and Its Implications,* London, 1970, Chapter 3.
4. J. Gonda., *Ancient Indian Kingship from the Religious Point of View,* Leiden 1969.
5. Burton Stein., *A History of India,* Delhi, 1998, p. 128.
6. Hermann Kulke., "The Early and Imperial Kingdom: a Processural Model of Integrative State Formation in Early Medieval India" in Hermann Kulke ed., *The State in India, 1000-1700 A.D.*, Delhi, 1995 pp.233-262.
7. R.S. Sharma., "Superstition and Politics" in Arthaśāstra of Kautilya" *The Journal of the Bihar Research Society,* vol. XL, 1954, pp. 223-231.
8. R. Shamsastry., *Kautilya's Arthaśāstra,* Mysore, 8th ed. 1967, Book XIII, 395, p. 434.
9. R.S. Sharma., *op.cit.*
10. S.D. Gyani., *Agnipurāṇa - A Study,* The Chowkhamba Studies, vol. XLII. Varanasi, 1964, p. 217; *Agnipurāṇa,* ch. 124.
11. *Agnipurāṇa,* ch. 136.
12. A. Eschmann., "Hinduization of Tribal Deities in Orissa" in *The Cult of Jagannath and Regional Tradition of Orissa,* ed. by A. Eschmann, H. Kulke, G.C. Tripathi, Delhi, 1978, pp 79-97.
13. C.J. Fuller., "Royal Divinity and Human Kingship in the Festivals of A South Indian Temple" in *South Asian Social Scientist,* 1985, 1, 3-43; *Purusottamamahatmya* of the *Skanda Purana* XI, pp. 125ff (1966); D. Shulman., *Tamil Temple Myths: Sacrifice and Divine Marriage in South Indian Saiva Tradition,* Princeton, 1980, pp. 40-55, Friedhelm Hardy., "Ideology and Cultural Contexts of the Srivaishnava Temple" in B.Stein ed. *South Indian Temples,* Delhi, 1978, pp. 119-152.
14. S.I.I. Vol. V Nos. 1010, 1031; *Epigraphia Andhrica,* vol. IV p. 47; Also see No. Mukunda Rao., *Kalinga Under the Eastern Gangas (Ca 900 A.D. to Ca 1200 A.D.)*, Delhi 1991, p. 65.
15. *S.I.I.* vol. IV 1347; *Ibid.*, vol. XVI, 48, 49, 150.

16. K.A.N. Sastri., *Colas,* Madras, 1975 p. 453.
17. *Ibid.*
18. Hans Bakker, ed., *The Sacred Centre as the Focus of Political Interest,* Groningen 1987, p. viii.
19. *Rukmāngada Charitra* (*Ēkādaśi Māhātmyam*), Vavilla, ed. Madras, 1924, Canto. III pp. 92-98.
20. *Ibid.*, v. 30.
21. *Ibid.*, v. 27.
22. *Ibid.*, v. 38.
23. *Ibid.*, v. 39.
24. *Āmuktamālyada,* Secunderabad, 1970, p. 118 v. 237; K. Satyanarayana., *A Study of the History and Culture of the Andhras*, Delhi, 1983, P. 289-291.
25. *S.I.I.* vol. X, nos. 665, 670, 666, 677, 681, 682, 684; *Ibid.*, vol. V, No. 1076.
26. K. Satyanarayana., *op.cit.*, p. 289.

13

Kings, Temples and Famines in Medieval Andhra

In the history of mankind that experienced the development of civilization language, family, religion and polity are certain evolutionary universals that have emerged and continued. It is observed that despite the commonality and universality of institutions, organizations, cultural patterns and values there have been significant variations in the internal dynamics, overt manifestations and inter linkages in different systems of society. In Andhra, royalty created a distinct system of values, norms, styles of life, institutions and patterns of hierarchical and distancing relationships. In the hereditary and monarchical form of government, the political power was ingrained and concentrated in the hands of the rulers revealing the all-pervasive power at mudane empirical level. On the other hand, while royalty was visible, religion was invisible and entirely based on faith and belief systems having omnipotent power. Both royalty and religion had tremendous impact on the lives of the people of Andhra society during the medieval times, irrespective of the ethnic diversities and caste hierarchy. Despite the observance of the principle of hereditary inheritance in obtaining the kingship, the acceptance of the royalty by the people was essential. In this context, religion helped legitimation of the bearer of the royalty and its acceptance by the people through certain religious ritual practices. This resulted in the development of state religion and motivated the kings of Andhra to build and donate to the temples, which was considered as a way of securing political legitimacy despite the development of distance between the royalty religion and that of common people. The "exclusiveness" and the "distinct form" of religious rituals observed by the royalty in respect of their entitlement to the privileged place in public participation and limited and occasional access to common people in places of worship of royalty was a part of the process of political legitimacy.[1] The construction of temples and its maintenance by the royalty through the donations besides the endowments made by the public ultimately led to the indirect contact of the royalty with the commoners.

During the medieval times the temples became powerful economic institutions meeting the requirements of the state and society through its administrative functionaries. The royal orders, appeal and instructions to the people were all inscribed on the temple walls with the intention of communicating the royal message to the people residing in remote areas also as the temples would be visited by them during the course of their pilgrimages. In the present chapter it is attemped to study the services offered by the royalty and state officials as well as the temples to the people in times of calamities such as famines and the desertion of villages. The efforts made by the royalty and the temples to mitigate the disastrous effect of both the natural and man-made calamities are subjected to empirical study through the inscriptions and literature of the medieval times. It is also attempted to describe the instances of famine as mentioned in the *Kaifiyats,* foreign accounts and literature with regard to the effects of famines on the people of the Andhra region and to highlight the concern of both the temples and the state for the welfare of the people.

Although the gods of the common people sometimes differ with those venerated by the *rajas*, the royalty used to patronize the Gods of different sects of Hinduism to gain the good will, favour and acceptance from the common folk. As a result, not only the gods of classical Hindu tradition were honoured and richly endowed with donations by the royalty but also encouraged the deification of local gods and their incorporation within the Hindu tradition. It is observed that the relationship between royalty, ritual and religion encompasses political, social psychological and economic dimensions making the life course an integral whole rather than divisive and segmental.[2] The policies of the state are sometimes changed and modified to suit the needs and requirements of the people keeping in view their sufferings and silent protests made through the desertion of the villages. Although far distant both in time and space, Kauṭilya's *Arthaśāstra,* an early work on statecraft, contain some useful information with regard to the role to be played by the kings in times of the occurrence of eight national calamities, of which reference has been made to the famines. During such times, Kauṭilya states that the king shall show favour to his people by providing them with seeds and provision (*bīja bhakto-pagraham*).[3] In this connection, he may either distribute his own collection of provisions or the hoarded income of the rich among the people or gain the support from his friends among the kings. It is also suggested by Kauṭilya that the king may migrate along with his subjects to another kingdom with abundant harvest. Further it is also stated that the king along with his people may settle near the sea shores, or the banks of the rivers or lakes so that he would be responsible to encourage his people to grow grains, vegetables, roots and fruits depending on the availability of water resources.[4] The king by way of hunting and fishing on a large scale may provide his subjects with wild beasts, birds, elephants, tigers and a variety of fishes. Thus theoretically it is stated in *Arthaśāstra* that the ideal king should come to the rescue of the people in case they are affected by the conditions of famine. The historical evidences examined in the present study reveal that in practice, the people as well as the officers like *karanams* who were entitled to enjoy the rights of the land-produce resulting from the *manya* lands assigned to them have left the places in times of severe famines in Andhra region.

In the work *Śrī Kālahastīmahātmyam* written by Dhurjati the conditions of famine are described in detail.[5] It is mentioned in the work as the famine that caused great distress (*kshāma mahā kshōbhaṁbu)* characterized by lack of rainfall (*varsha sūnyamu*) and hot sunshine. The lack of rainfall has disturbed greatly the hearts of the people, as there were no thunders and signs of clouds in the sky. As a result, there were no sufficient crops to provide food for the people and hence they had resorted to change their food habits as they were forced to eat the rice of inferior quality including *veduru biyyamu,* large bulbous roots and tubers (*gotte chetlu, injetlu*) and the pulp of the date palm trees (*īta gumju*).[6] Some people tried to sow millets (*gaṁṭe*) as it would give the yield within sixty days by watering the fields through the device of *ētam*. But these water-lifting devices got spoiled and not functioned, as they were not in use for a long period.[7] Having been attacked by the bad effects of the planets Śani and Mīna, people became highly impoverished and very thin without much flesh due to lack of sufficient food and the hungry stricken people left the places leaving behind their wives and children in search of food.[8] Many people died due to lack of food in large numbers while some people abandoned the places and went to foreign lands to find out livelihood. The seriousness of the situation was so desperate that people have resorted to cannibalism (*mānisi mānisi dinu karavu*).[9] These literary references reveal the knowledge of the writer with regard to the conditions of famine and the sufferings of the people. Further it is also important to note here the cause and effect established by the writer between the changes in the planetary positions and the conditions of famine as it suggests prevlence of the superstitious beliefs that were prevalent and propagated by the literate of the society intentionally.

The temple economies are strengthened during the medieval times with the liberal donations and endowments made by the rich and common people. As a result the gods became wealthy and prosperous and were decorated with costly jewels and ornaments made of gold and silver. But the temple managements bestowed greater attention and care towards its clientele i.e., the devotees. Therefore, whenever the people were suffering, the temples came to the rescue of the people in fulfilling their needs. Although no specific information is contained in the inscriptions of the Andhra region about the famines and its aftermath, it can be gathered from the neighbouring Tamil region one specific reference with regard to the help rendered by the temples during the period of great famine. From an inscription found on the South wall of Rajendra Cholesvara temple at Ilayangudi dated in the 11th regnal year of *Tribhuvana Chakravartin* Sundara Pandyadeva it is known that the temple superintendent (*tanattar*) agreed to burn a perpetual lamp before the god in lieu of 110 *paṇam* received by them as endowment from Marudidamgondan-sigalivendam.[10] In this connection, it is interesting to note that the amount of 110 *paṇam* was utilized by the *tānāttar* for the purpose of restoring to the god some ornaments which they had sold in the 10th regnal year of the king and utilized the proceeds to tide over a famine (*kshāma*). This reveals that the temple management, to provide some financial help to the needy people who were affected by famine, utilized the ornaments of the god. Due to the severity of the famine conditions sometimes people also lost their freedom and liberty. To obtain food during the famines, the people had to suffer. It is known from an inscription of 13th century A.D. that the people sold their personal liberty during a famine to obtain food.[11] Although such instances might be many depending on the nature and intensity of famines we could get a very limited number of epigraphical references in this direction. However, it is known from the account of a Portuguese chronicler, Joao de Castro about a devastating famine that occurred during A.D. 1540 which reduced many of the inhabitants of several villages of the eastern districts to cannibalism.[12] As a result of this severe famine it is stated that two thirds of the population perished. Due to the severity of the famine people of the villages including *agraharas* migrated en masse to the neighbourhood areas.[13] Further the effects of famines can be noticed from the sale of lands and villages and the changes brought about in the ownership rights of the lands. The sales and purchases of land affected during a severe famine are referred to in a Local Record.[14] According to it, Bellamkonda *Sīma* including a number of villages was affected by famine in 1402 A.D. as a result of which many villagers left their place and returned after a lapse of a few years. Another famine occurred in the same region which existed for a long span of time i.e., 12 years (1442-1454).[15] In view of the undesirable conditions that prevailed in the area some of the villages were sold at a very low price. It is mentioned that two villages Konda Kavur and Gurujepalli were sold for 160 *varahas,* each valued at 80 *varahas*. But after the restoration of the conditions to normalcy those who sold and left the villages came back and expelled the occupants and challenged the ownership of some land pushing the state to confusion. As a result of these land disputes the state was deprived of its land revenue. The *Kaifiyats* of Guntur district contain references to the famine that occurred in the Bellamkondasima that covers villages Nandigama and Chilukuru. It is mentioned in the *Kaifiyat* that the famine prevailed for 12 years and it is stated as *Ravudri saptakam* and *Prabava paṁchakam* after the name of the years. In view of the severe conditions of famine in the villages Konidembaka Narapa Raju sold the *mirāsi* rights of two villages for 90 *varahas* and left the place.[16] The people in the village Bhimavaram of the Bellamkonda Sima also felt the effects of the same famine. It is stated in another *Kaifiyat* that the *mirāsi* rights of the village Bhimavaram were sold by

Konidembaka Surapa Raju for 60 *varahas* to Mantriraju Mantraya, who was the *karanam* of the village Koduru and left the village.[17] It is stated in the *Kaifiyats* of the villages Kasuvukurru and Kattempudi of Guntur district that the temple services were disrupted and there were no regular *archanas* and other temple rituals due to the occurrence of the famines.[18] Thus we could get some information from the local records about the effects of famine on ownership right of lands and villages as well as on the temple services.

Besides such horrifying disastrous famines, the mass migratory movements of the people that resulted during the Vijayanagara period exemplify the silent protestations made by the people to pay excess taxes imposed on them by the state. The kings when they were informed of the illegal and burdensome taxes collected by the state officials had responded favourably with the view to provide a helping hand to the people.[19] As a result the kings issued the *Nammika sasanam* or *Nammika kaul* announcing the remission of certain taxes to the people who deserted the villages in the Vijayanagara state.[20] Likewise certain privileges and concessions were offered to the people to encourage them to come back and resettle in the abandoned villages. The concern of the royalty can also be noticed through the assurance grants (*abhaya sasanam*) issued in favour of merchants and traders of both inland and foreign countries.[21] Particularly the Motupalli inscription of Kakatiya ruler Ganapati deva and the Reddi king Anavota granted to the merchants coming to trade at Motupalli refer to various tax concessions accorded to them.

Although direct information is not forthcoming from the historical sources, it can be assumed that the temple priests, kings, the royal preceptors (*raja gurus)*, astrologers and soothsayers might have played an important role to mitigate the disastrous effects of the natural calamities through propagating and spreading certain religious and superstitious beliefs among the people to build up confidence in them so that they would not easily abandon the villages in search of new villages.

Attributing the cause of famine to the changes in planetary positions reveal how the superstitious religious beliefs are publicized among people. The role played by the village deities as the protector goddess of the villagers in this context was immense, particularly in the case of calamities like epidemic diseases and famines. The local or village deities were the deities of the common people that reveal a great diversity and generally they are local contextual and not part of the 'Great Traditions'. But it is observed that in course of time the contextual faiths at micro level enlarged the classical universalistic religious systems by opening up the possibility of encompassing the deities within the traditions. Due to such encompassing processes the community character was strengthened at local level despite the caste and religious distinctions and diversities. Thus it can be seen that the natural calamities and disasters sometimes bring integrity not only among the people but also establish good linkages among the people, state and religious centres that create unification and integration at certain level of generality amidst diversities at both micro and macro levels.

References

1. N.K. Singhi, Rajendra Joshi ed., *Religion, Ritual and Royalty,* Jaipur, Delhi 1999 p. 10-11; J.C. Heesterman., *The Inner Conflict of Tradition,* Chicago, 1985.
2. Hermann Kulke., *The State in India 1000-1700 A.D.* Delhi, 1995 pp. 233-262; Cynthia Talbot., *Precolonial India in Practice: Society, Religion and Identity in Medieval Andhra,* Delhi, 2001; Also see Hall Kenneth R., *Structure and Society in Early South India; Essays in Honour of Noboru Karashima*, Delhi, 2001.
3. R. Shamasastri., Kautilya's *Arthasastra,* chapter, III, p. 237, Mysore, eighth edition, 1967.
4. *Ibid.*
5. *Sri Kalahastimahatmyam,* ed. by PSR Appa Rao, A.P. Sahitya Academy, Hyderabad, 1968, Canto III, p. 104, v. 148-156.
6. *Ibid.*, v. 150.
7. *Ibid.*, v. 152.
8. *Ibid.*, v. 153.

9. *Ibid.*, v. 156.
10. *A.R.* 291 of 1950.
11. *A.R.* No. 53 of 1899; A.R. 29 of 1911.
12. *Indian Antiquary* 1923 p. 232; Also see K. Satyanarayana., *A Study of the Hisotry and Culture of the Andhras,* Delhi, 1983 vol. II, p. 347.
13. *Ibid.*
14. *Mack. Local Records,* M. 387, pp. 77-89; K. Satyanarayana., *op.cit.,* p. 350-351.
15. *Ibid.*
16. Guntur District village Kaifiyats IVth Part, Hyderabad, 1990, pp. 171-174.
17. *Ibid.*, pp. 198.
18. *Kaifiyats of Guntur District, Part III,* p. 14-16 and 11-12, Hyderabad, 1988.
19. M. Krishna Kumari., *Studies on Medieval Andhra Hisotry and Culture,* Delhi, 1994, p. 81.
20. M. Krishna Kumari., *Facets of Andhra Culture,* Delhi, 1999, p. 66.
21. M. Krishna Kumari, *Sermons from Stones-Contribution of Andhra to Art, Culture and Thought,* Delhi, 2002, p. 76.

14

ROYALTY, WOMEN AND THE VRATAMS IN MEDIEVAL ANDHRA

Women play a major role in the continuation of the religious and ritual traditions in India in general and Andhra in particular. The religious observances such as fasting on certain auspicious days and festivals followed by women are mainly intended for obtaining religious merit (*punya*) for themselves as well as for the well-being of their family members. Besides these, certain rituals are especially prescribed in the ancient texts to be followed by women so that they will be blessed with material wealth and prosperity. The Telugu stone inscriptions of medieval Andhra provide good information about the liberal patronage extended by women in setting up several types of *bhogams* and *prasadams* in offering the ritual services to the gods in the temples. '*Vrat'* is a ritual cum religious fasting on religious occasions in worship of various Hindu gods and goddesses. *Vratas* are a kind of practice of penance and observance of austerities prescribed for women either through tradition or the literary texts. It is generally believed that the benefit of the performance of *vratas* comes to either the person who observed them or to the person for whom it is observed. The severe penance and fasting observed by Pārvati to obtain lord Śiva as her husband has been set as an ideal example for women to encourage them to practise the *vratas*. Although there were several *vratas* followed by women during the medieval times, only some of them were mentioned in the inscriptions. To inspire and encourage the women folk to observe the *vratas* deliberate attempts were made by the elite of the patriarchal society. To strengthen their views in this context they resorted to connect most of the stories of the *vratas* with the Purāṇic legends and mythological stories. However, sometimes the local gods and goddesses are also worshipped while observing the *vratams*. The entire ritual includes fasting, worshipping gods or goddesses narrating the stories of the merits of the *vratams* and giving away gifts or donations. The *vratams* common for the genders include fasting on the occasion of festivals and holy days like *Sivaratri, Janmashthami, Ekadasi, Nagula Chaviti, Sravna Somavara* etc. Besides these *vratas* commonly followed by all the Hindus, different *vratas* are practised by the Saivites and Vaishnavites depending on their sectarian faiths. However, there are certain other *vratas*, which are exclusively observed by women/girls. The impact of the royalty can be felt on the socio-religious life of the people, irrespective of their ethnic diversities and caste hierarchy. By encouraging and patronizing the performance of rituals like the *vratas* in a well-defined manner the royalty had exercised its powers that are visible and all pervasive at mundane empirical level. With the support obtained from the royalty the elaborate procedures observed in the practice of *vratas* gained sanctity and by the adherence to the rules and conditions prescribed for them, they assigned significant meanings and helped in conveying meanings to the nature and quality of relationship. An attempt is made here to analyse the *vratas* and their related stories mentioned in the historical sources to explore the relationship between the legendary stories construed in connection with the *vratas* and the status of women in the patriarchal society. It is also intended to focus on the women's space in religious rituals as well as their attitude towards such practices and the role of royalty in observing the *vratas* during the medieval times in Andhra. The Telugu poets exclusively wrote extolling the religious merits and significance of the *vratas*. To this category belong the literary works of Mallana and Srinatha entitled *Rukmāngada Charitra* alias *Ēkādaśi Māhātmyam* and *Śivarātri Māhātmyam,* respectively. These works and other literary works like *Nāchikētō-pākhyānamu* refer to the characteristic features of the women as *pativratas* and the merits of possessing great devotion to their husbands (*pati bhakti*). Besides these literary works, stray references to the names of the *vratas* collected from the inscriptions of Andhra form the major sources for the study of the *vratas,* their observance and patronage extended to certain *vratas* by the royalty during the medieval times.

The relationship between royalty, religion and rituals is highly integrative rather than segmental or divisive. When the common people perform certain *vratas* for their own merit or for the common good and welfare of the people of the kingdom, the kings used to support the *vratins* and also the performers of the *vratas*. There is an interesting inscription of an Eastern Chalukyan king Ammaraja II's time referring to the quasi-religious custom prevalent in that period known as *karpati vrata*. The government epigraphist has reported that it was a vow of poverty observed by a *bahmachārin* during Amma's time.[1] However, the circumstances that led to the granting of a village by the king Amma II to the Brahmin *brahmachārin* Paṇḍiyaśarman described in the inscription provides some more information about *karpati vrata*. It is observed that *Karpati vrata* was performed by the Brahmins of well disciplined minds for the welfare of their royal masters, sometimes voluntarily and sometimes at their bidding, whenever the latter were in a state of difficulties or ill-health, or for the success of any military expedition undertaken in a distant country. It is mentioned in the record that Paṇḍiya Śarman, son of Guṇḍa Śarman and grandson of Pāliya Peddiya of the *Bharadvāja gōtra* and *yājñavalkya śākha* was an inhabitant of Kalavatorra and is described as "one who was in the investigation of the proper behaviour and conduct" (*samāchāra vichāra nishṭitaḥ*) and one who performed the *karpati vrata.* Paṇḍiya Śarman was a *brahmachārin* and a loyal servant of the king. The king Ammarāja, being pleased with his devotion and in order to release him from the necessity of continuing the *karpati vrata* granted him the village of Padamkaluru in the Pennatavadi *Vishaya,* as an *agrahāra* on the occasion of a lunar eclipse, so that he might settle down as a peaceful householder (*grihastha*).[2] Another reference to the observance of *karpati vrata* during Amma's period is noticed from a copper plate record. It is known from this record that Kākartya Gundana, one of the progenitors of the Kākatīya rulers was a feudal chieftain and ruled over Nātavādi *Vishaya* during Amma's reign.[3] A follower of this chieftain was a certain Dommana Śarman, who for a long observed the most difficult religious rite, called *karpati vrata* in order to please his master. Although the occasion for the observance of this *vrata* is not stated in the copper plate record, it seems that the *vrata* requires the observer to be a *brahmacharin,* practising continuous celibacy, bathing early every day, speaking truth, preserving purity of mind and body, compassion, forbearance, liberality, kindness and practising the prescribed details. After the close of the *vrata,* the feudal chieftain Kaktiya Gundana requested king Rājādhirāja Rājamahēndra who was pleased to grant the village of Mangallu in the Nātavāḍi *Vishaya* in the Nandigama Taluk, Krishna District as an *agrahāra* to Dommana *brahmachārin,* on the occasion of a certain winter solstice with the libation of water and granted it by exempting all kinds of taxes (*sarvakari parihāra*).

In the socio-religious life of women, *vratas* form an integral part. The *vratas* are observed for the well-being of father, brother, son, husband, etc., and all male kins. This could be understood in the traditional social setting in India in which at different stages of their life women remain under the patronage/protection of males i.e., father/brother during childhood or youth, followed by husband and finally in the event of the death of her husband, of their sons. Since women did not have direct access to the economic resources and proprietary rights as per the *dharma śāstras,* it is believed that it is in the interests of all women to wish for the continued well-being of her male protectors. In this context, it is considered that the observance of *vratas* and obtaining the favours/boons from the gods were the main objectives of the women. Quite often the *vratas* are accompanied with songs, festivity and rejoicing. This can be noticed from the literary sources wherein the collective participation, performance and sharing of the different dimensions of the *vratas* observed by the women are described in detail. The collective performance of the *vratas* help in the continuance and reinforcement of the *vratas* besides providing gaiety and opportunity for women to shed boredom from routine domestic chores. It is evident from the literary sources that the observance of the *vratas* was a socially approved manner of religious practice that conferred virtue on the fasting woman, merit as well as long life and happiness on her male relatives. It may be pointed out here as observed by other social scientists that in the case of the women her penances (*tapas*) are always for her husband, while the asceticism of a man takes him towards his own personal goal.[4] The *vratas* generally help in either reinforcing or promoting the patriarchal cultural values of society as most of the stories of the *vratas* treated women as having a subordinate status, with their lives rotating around the husband, son and brother/father i.e., all the male members of the family for whom she observes the *vratas* with great devotion.[5] In this context it is important to mention here that there are no fasts or *vratas* observed for the well-being and long life of the daughters, wives and mothers.

In many of the literary texts the central theme is that the pious wife, who faces all manners of affliction on behalf of her spouse or his family and succeeds in gaining divine blessing for her husband's longevity through worshipping a particular deity in a prescribed manner. The characteristic features of a *pativrata* are mentioned in *Rukmangada Charitra.*[6] It is stated that the wife shall never think of anyone else except her husband and shall treat and obey her husband's words as the Vedic hymns and serve her relatives from her husband's side with great devotion.[7] She shall never leave her husband and her devotion to him and shall indulge seriously in observing the *vratas*, fasting, visit pilgrim centres and worship the gods.[8] Any deviation in practice from this rule will push her into hell. The merits and power of wifely devotion (*pativrata*) to her husband are extolled by stating that a woman who shows devotion to her husband will obtain the great and supernatural powers of the Gandharvas, Siddhas and Vidyadharas besides obtaining good wealth and prosperity.[9] While comparing the socio-religious status of the married women with that of the widows, it is described that a woman will be considered auspicious and prosperous when her husband is alive and when she is adorned with bridal chain (*mangala sutra*) on her neck.[10] Her status is perceived as the most important and desirable state so long as her husband is alive. The wife has no social existence or life without her husband in this world. Great importance is attached to the longevity of her husband and this is because of the Hindu traditional ideology that a woman ceases to be a wife without her husband and that she ceases to be a person in the society. The literary texts also eulogise and immortalize the position of the woman who commits Sati. It is stated that if a woman ends her life after the death of her husband, she will be received by the divine beings and *apsaras* in the Heaven.[11] Similar type of references are also noticed in another work, *Nachiketopakhyanamu* written by Daggupalli Duggana. While describing the nature and characteristic features of *punya pativrata* it is stated that the divine beings will shower their blessings on her with flowers after her death in the world of Heaven and she will be welcomed by several *Vidyadharas*.[12] From these writings it is evident that it is generally viewed by the people that a wife's devotion to her husband is considered as highly meritorious than the devotion to the God and that her position in the society with her husband was the most important and highly desirable state in a woman's entire life. Therefore, the longevity of a husband for which a wife performs several rituals and *vratas* is not only an emotionally but also a socially desirable state for the wife's continued existence as a socially acceptable individual.

Since medieval times, devotionalism became a constitutive part of Hinduism and it was developed within the hierarchical and institutional frame works of popular Hinduism. Generally the ideal Hindu woman is symbolized by auspicious Lakshmi, who, as the consort of lord Vishnu, is commonly represented as the perfect woman and wife, although there are many goddesses, who also exemplify the virtuous "*pativrata*" (devoted to her husband).[13] The Puranic woman like Savitri, who was so devoted to her husband (*pativrata*) that she followed him after his death into the underworld and was successful finally in compelling Yama, the lord of Death, to release him. A close examination of the literary works reveal that deliberate attempts have been made by the elite of the society to inspire the women to be more subservient and docile in the household and to be committed as well as devoted to their husbands by emulating the examples of the *pativratas* like Sītā, Sāvitrī, Arundhatī and the women who committed *Sati*. In that process, even in the case of a woman who has a wicked husband, social norms have traditionally emphasised that a Hindu wife's salvation lies in serving her husband devotedly in this life and earthly world. The legendary stories and the *vrata kathas* demonstrate the model example of the *pativrata's* devotion to her husband, that calls for a woman to think only of the happiness and welfare of her husband to the extent of subordinating and subsuming her own feelings and needs. It is generally held that a woman by adhering herself to the moral values and husbandly devotion protects her husband through her piety, purity of thought and action. The *vrata kathas* nurture the traditional ideology of *pativrata,* by incorporating the basic Hindu values of realization and helps to perpetuate the patriarchal structure by making the personal goals of woman fit the structural needs.[14] To a large extent, the *vratams* performed by the devoted wife nurtures such an ideology. For example, *Arundhatī vratam* is mainly intended for women only. The family woman observes this *vratam* for freedom from widowhood and for begetting male progeny and she observes it on the third *tithi* in the beginning of the spring (*vasanta*) season.[15] In this *vrata* prayers are offered to Arundhatī, the wife of sage Vasishtha, who is well known for her great virtues. Hēmādri refers to this *vrata* in his work and describes its merits for obtaining the male progeny and ensuring a long life to the husband of a woman who observes the *vrata.*[16]

The other important *vratas* mentioned in the inscriptions are *Lakshmīnārāyana Vratam, Jalaśayana Vratam, Asūnyasayyā Vratam* and *Asita Dvādasī Vratam.* The Bodpur inscription states that Kuppāṁbika, wife of Malayāla ejuṇḍa Dandaṇātha, performed all these *vratas.*[17] All these *vratas* have a specified day and month and all these are calendaric and seasonal. Of the *vratams* mentioned above the first three *vratams* are intended to worship lord Viṣhnu and Lakshmī. *Lakshmīnārāyaṇa Vratam* is performed on every full day in a month commencing from the full moon day of *Phālguṇa* in respect of Lakshmī and Nārāyaṇa. *Jalaśayana Vratam* is meant for the worship of Vishnu while Vishnu remains in water on the 14th day of the dark fortnight in the month of *Kārttika.* In case of *Asūnya Sayyā Vratam* lord Hari and Lakshmi will be worshipped for four months starting from the 2nd day of the dark fortnight of *Śrāvana* to ensure long life for both husband and wife. *Asitasita Dvādasī Vratam* will be performed on the 12th lunar day of either dark or bright fortnight. For the observance of these *vratas,* the *vratins* are supposed to refrain from consuming food altogether or to limit themselves to eat only certain type of food items before sunrise. Special types of food items are to be prepared to offer them to the gods and goddesses.

The *vratas* and the associated rituals performed mostly by women and sometimes in association with their husbands became an integral part of women's lives. It is important to note that the observance of the *vratams* at the household level does not generally require the services of the male Brahmin priests and that it is exclusively the arena of the women. The performance of the *vratams* is marked by collective performance and collective action by the women by way of offering songs, recital of *vrata kathas* and other ritual services in which the family women act as "doers". The veneration of the gods through the religious observance of the *vratams* is thus different from their regular worship at public places i. e., temples in which the male Brahmin priests act as intermediaries between the gods and devotees. The religious observance of the *vratas* was viewed by the Andhra women of the medieval times as both a religious duty and a traditional obligation on the part of an ideal wife. From the sources examined it is evident that the women of the medieval times did not consider that the *vratas* were imposed on them and that they were forced to perform the religious austerities for the good and welfare of their husbands in the patriarchal society. On the other hand, the legendary stories constructed on the religious merits of the performance of the *vratas* confirms the traditional view that women play a key role in the observance of the *vratas* as the doers of the rituals. Further they inspire and encourage the women to perform them for the longevity of their husbands and to obtain divine blessings. For the continuation of religious traditions and rituals, women play an active role through their devotion to their husbands and the gods. Although some of the *vratams* discussed above were totally forgotten and are not regularly practised by the women during the modern period due to the changes in the life styles of the people, it is observed that the basic concepts and the ideology of the *vratams* and their socio-religious significance did not alter totally through the passage of time. The ritual practice of observance of the *vratams* was both a part of religious norms and ceremonialities of the women folk. In response to the changes during the different temporal periods in history the concept of the *vratams* got sustained and manifested itself in well-formed customs and practices both in the sacred and non-sacred realms of lives. Besides the *vratams* observed by women, it is evident from the inscriptional evidence discussed above that the *vratams* were patronized by the royalty for their welfare as well as for the good of the people of the society.

References

1. *Subject Index to the Annual Report on Indian Epigraphy,* Delhi, 1988, p. 70; A.R. 1917, 24.
2. *Indian Antiquary,* vol. VII, p. 17; B.V. Krishna Rao., *History of the Eastern Chalukyas of Vengi,* Hyderabad, 1973, pp. 295-296.
3. Copper plate no. 1 of *A.R.* 1916-17. *A.R.E.* 117-118.
4. Veena Das., "Mythological Film and Its Framework of Meaning" in *India International Quarterly,* vol. 8, Number 1, 1981, p.43.
5. Varsha Joshi and Rima Hooja., "Vrat and Vrata Kathas: Ritual, Women and Patriarchy" in N.K. Singh, Rajendra Joshi ed. *Religion, Ritual and Royalty,* Jaipur, 1999, pp. 198-199.
6. Malana's *Rukmangada Charitra,* Madras, 1924, pp. 161-166, canto IV.
7. *Ibid.,* Canto IV, v. 81.
8. *Ibid.,* Canto IV, v. 84.
9. *Ibid.,* Canto IV, v. 95.
10. *Ibid.*, Canto IV, v. 90-91.
11. *Ibid.*, Canto IV, v. 94-96.
12. Dagupalli Duggana's *Nachiketopakhyanamu,* p.141, v. 177, 178.
13. C.J. Fuller., *The Camphor of Flame,* Delhi, 1992, p. 202.
14. V. Dhruvarajan., *Hindu Women and Power of Ideology,* New Delhi, 1989, p. 99; Tanika Sarkar and Urvasi Butalia (eds)., *Women and the Hindu Right: Collection of Essays,* Kali for Women, New Delhi, 1995, p. 332.
15. *Hyderabad Archaeological Series* 13-50; Kunduri Iswardut., *Inscriptional Glossary of Andhra Pradesh,* Hyderabad, 1967, p. 25.
16. Heamdri., *Chaturvarga Chintamani,* Vrata Khanda, vol. II, pp. 312-315.
17. *Hyderabad Archaeological Series,* 13-50.

15

Robbery and Royalty in Medieval Andhra: Some Historical Insights

In the history of mankind family, religion, language and polity are certain evolutionary universals that have emerged and continued through the historical process, irrespective of the internal variations and roles played by them through time and space. For the material wealth and well-being, people struggle hard during different temporal periods in history and their attempts to hoard and amass their wealth resulted in obtaining the possession of fixed assets in the form of agricultural lands or villages besides saving their wealth in the manner of the collection of the precious metals like gold, silver coins, jewellery, gems, etc., of high purchasing value. The wealth and prosperity attained by the people in the society naturally draws the attention of the thieves, a professional class of people, whose activities are mainly stealing, theft and attacking the people while they are travelling through the highways, waterways, forests and hilly tracts or when they are stationed at their homes. Since the activities of the robbers cause great misery, pain and loss of wealth to the people, robbery is considered as one of the various social evils from the ancient period. Despite the fact that robbery was abhorred and mentioned in the *dharmaśāstra* literature as a crime punishable by death, a small segment of people in the society depended wholly on these activities and preferred to aspire for the wealth acquired by the others, which fact was considered as one of the seven vices during the medieval times. Unlike the other aspects that can be known through the good number of inscriptional and literary sources, the inscriptional sources for the study of robbery and theft are very meagre. Rarely, such instances are referred to in the stone inscriptions and none of the copper plate grants mention any cases of robbery during the medieval period. On the other hand, the Telugu literary works provide some useful information on this issue and some works describe not only the activities of the thieves but also the impacts of the robbery on the victims also. As no detailed survey of the historical sources on the theme of the social evil robbery in medieval Andhra has been attempted so far, it is endeavored to probe into the life style of the robbers, their *modus operandi,* the equipment used to steal things, the punishments imposed on the offenders and the duties of the king in this connection, on the basis of the Telugu literary works such as Mallana's *Rukmāngada Charitra,*[1] Ketana's *Vijñānēśvarīyam,*[2] Koravi Goparaju's *Siṁhāsana Dvātriṁśaka,*[3] Krishnadevaraya's *Āmuktamālyada,*[4] Sankara Kavi's *Hariśchandrōpākhyānamu,*[5] Tenali Rama Krishna's *Pāṅduranga Māhātmyamu,*[6] and Sarangu Tammaya's *Vaijayantī Vilāsamu.*[7]

In *Haṁsaviṁśati* of Ayyalaraju Narayanamatya of 17th century, robbery was mentioned as one of the sixty-four *kaḷas.*[8] It is interesting to note here that it was not mentioned as one of the sixty-four arts in the Telugu literary work *Siṁhāsana Dvātriṁśaka* datable to 15th century A.D. What transpired the writers of the 17th century to include robbery in the arts to be learnt by the *brahmachārins* while pursuing their education is difficult to ascertain. Probably the socio-economic conditions that prevailed in the Andhradesa of 17th century

A.D. might have necessitated the incorporation of robbery as one of the subjects to be learnt while acquiring knowledge and proficiency in sixty-four arts. This can be suggested on the basis of the evidence that not only the robbery but also the learning of some other subjects like the preparation of the alcoholic drinks (*maīrēyamu kūrchuta*), hunting (*vēṭa*), betting (*jūdamu*) are included in the long list of the sixty-four arts in the same work, which are generally considered as the seven vices that are to be avoided by the people in the society.

In Āndhradēśa, royalty created a distinct system of values, norms, styles of life, institutions and patterns of hierarchical relationships in accordance with the principles laid own in the *dharmaśāstra* literature and works on polity (*rājanīti*). In the monarchical hereditary form of rule, power was ingrained and the king was considered as the chief of justice. It is the duty of the kings to protect and safeguard the interests of the people and, in that sense, the royalty was visible, more effective and had all pervasive power at mundane-empirical level and sometimes when there were not physical evidences to punish the culprits, the kings used to exercise the power based on faith and belief systems which had a tremendous impact on the judgements delivered. The honour associated with royalty strengthened by the legitimization through religious practices had a profound impact in the maintenance of righteousness (*dharma*) in the lives of the people and on the restoration of law and order in the society. However, it may be observed here that the fines and punishments imposed on the culprits for the same kind of offence vary in accordance with caste hierarchy. In this context it may be mentioned that while robbery was treated as a serious offence punishable by death according to Daṇḍi's *Daśakumāra Charitra,*[9] in practice a different situation is noticed from some of the Telugu literary works of the period. Sarangu Tammayya mentions in his work, *Vaijayantī Vilāsamu* that the *dharmāsana* has decided Vipranarayana as a thief who has stolen a silver vessel from the temple and imposed the punishment of sending him away from the territory (*Sīmā*) as per the prescriptions of the law laid down in *Vijñānēśvarīyam* which states that tonsure of the hair, expelling the culprit from the temple service and that no brahmin should be killed despite the serious offence committed by them.[10]

In *Rukmāngada Charitra* it is mentioned that the family life of good people will be disrupted due to the thieves and hence the kings should govern the kingdom in such a manner that he should set aside all the fears and apprehensions of the people due to robbery.[11] If the king was kind towards the thieves the people would suffer greatly and, therefore, future king was advised not to be kind towards the thieves.[12] Further it is stated in the same work that, if any officer attempts to stop the king when he was attacking a group of thieves, such officers should be sent away immediately.[13]

The life-style of the robbers can be gleaned through the works—*Simhāsana Dvātrimśaka* and *Hariśchandrōpākhyānamu.* In *Simhāsana Dvātrimśaka* it is described that the thieves wear black clothes and besmear their bodies with ashes so that they cannot easily be recognized while they move about in the streets during night. They carry with them, when they go out on their job, the instruments like a large hook that resembles the nail of an eagle (*gradda gōru*), a small box holding insects, a ball with thorns, sedatives, scissors with a wooden handle, a small sword, black powder, etc.[14] The tools and the other paraphernalia of the robbers carried along with them were all required for their job to enter into the houses without causing any disturbance to the sleep of the inmates of the house or even to break the walls or to stupefy the people, so that they could carry out their work without any hindrance. The small insects carried by them seem to be for the purpose of blowing off the lamps in the house to make it darker. For the lifting of the valuables through the small holes and to make holes in the walls of the houses depending on the needs, the robbers carried with them several instruments and tools. Probably in anticipation of the resistance from the victims, the robbers must have carried swords and daggers. In the work

Hariśchandrōpākhyānamu, Sankara Kavi describes the manner in which the thief enters into the royal palace, where the prince was sleeping. He mentions that the thief entered into the palace after making a hole in the wall without causing much noise and robbed the valuable jewelry worn by the prince on his ears, neck and hands who was in a deep sleep.[15] In the same work it is mentioned that the thief entered the palace with great courage wearing a small black cloth tied around his loins, footwear that would make no noise at all, a ball of thorns, a sword and some other instruments. In understanding the lifestyles and type of dress worn by the thieves the descriptions given in the work *Āmuktamālyada* are of great value. It describes the thief as wearing a loin cloth tightly around his waist, a large moustache, a small rounded belly, the face besmeared with ashes, a mark made with wax as a dot and a sword in his hand to attack the people.[16] In the same manner Tenali Ramakrishna in his work, *Pāṇḍuranga Māhātmyam* gave a detailed description of a group of thieves who attacked the pedestrians in the forest tract. It mentions that the thieves fell on the people all of a sudden and attacked them with the sword that they carry along with them and stolen the valuables held by the people. The jewelry carried by the Brahmin Nigama Śarmā, which he in turn had stolen from his house was thus robbed by the thieves on the wayside.[17]

Besides the tools and weapons carried by the thieves when they go out for their job in the darkness of the nights, the tactics and strategies observed by the robbers when they steal things are described in detail in *Āmuktamālyada*. It refers to the close observations made by the thieves before they actually attack the people on the wayside. From these descriptions it is evident that the thieves consider that the preliminary survey of the surroundings followed by careful planning and its execution are the essential prerequisites for their success in stealing. In the same work it is mentioned how a Brahmin has earned the money in a short span of time by resorting to various practices, which were not generally advisable for the Brahmins and treated as unethical means of procuring wealth and has drawn the attention of the thieves due to his ambitious nature.[18] In that context, it refers to how the Brahmin inter-dined with the other Brahmins who were socially ostracized for the sake of money that could be gained from it, how he received the *dānas* (gifts) of inferior quality and how he saved the money by eating very little and sometimes resorting to the practice of eating the food offered on the occasion of the annual death ceremonies. The amount gained through all such means was given by the brahmin to the merchants with the intention of getting interest on that money besides selling the rice collected by him from the people after the performance of several types of rituals. All these things were carefully watched and observed by the thieves who followed the Brahmin in the village from time to time.[19] Further the way how the Brahmin has hurriedly made the preparations for his journey to his native place after collecting the money and valuables from the merchants were observed by the thieves and accordingly they planned to rob the brahmin on the way. The thief accompanied the Brahmin in the disguise of a traveller holding a bag in his hands. On their way the thief gave the wrong directions and led the people to the forest. When all the passengers believed the thief as their co-passenger and followed him to the way leading to the forest, the thief gave a signal to his fellow thieves by blowing a long whistle and immediately stones fell upon all the passengers from four directions and the thieves attacked the people with arrows. Despite the fact that some people resisted the attack of the thieves most of the people ran hither and thither throwing away all their belongings on the floor and left the place. Some were seriously wounded while some pleaded the thieves to show some mercy on them and that they would give some money and valuables to them and further requested them not to touch their ladies.[20] When some persons hid themselves behind the bushes, the thieves threw spears and arrows in the direction of the bushes. The thieves made the people even to leave their clothes and, in turn, they offered them small loin clothes. The thieves examined and searched thoroughly the people, the bags, hair and even the soles of the footwear and thus robbed them completely. The thieves snatched the moneybag carried away by the Brahmin and they did not even leave the golden ear ornaments of the Brahmin while they left the place. When the brahmin threatened the thieves while they are leaving the place, the thieves came back again and wounded him severely with the fear that if the brahmin revealed their whereabouts, to either the king or the Reddi they would kill them.[21] The tactics and skills of the robbers are described in detail in *Siṁhāsana Dvātriṁśaka* in connection with the theft conducted at the residence of the princess. In this context, it is mentioned that the thieves before approaching and entering into the house of the princess, listened to all the sounds without themselves making any noise, hiding themselves at the corners and finally entered into the palace by throwing the medicines that make the people to lose their consciousness and also throwing ashes on those who were alert at that time.[22] To reach the palace where the princess resides, they had to cut down a hole in the wall to enter. Thus it refers to the various movements and the *modus operandi* observed by the thieves in stealing valuables.

The agony and suffering of the victims attacked by the thieves are described in detail in the work, *Āmuktamālyada*[23]. Besides the loss of property and valuables, sometimes the victims were severely wounded by the highway robbers. It is stated that the people who were badly hurt were in search of a physician who could attend to them for some first aid services to their wounds. Some people who need some surgery to their wounds moved restlessly holding tightly the cuts to arrest the outflow of the blood from the wounds. Some people were holding a burnt cloth against the wounds caused on their heads and requesting for rice porridge to refresh themselves. It is described that some people were giving clothes from the sarees they had, to tie up the wounds caused by the swords while some others were explaining their losses to their friends and relatives and seeking their help and support. Thus the effect of highway robberies are graphically narrated in the work that reveals the suffering undergone by the people due to the attack of the robbers.

To discourage the people who resort to the practice of robbery, the punishments imposed on such crimes were made severe and sometimes even the capital punishment was also referred to in the literary works. *Vijñānēśvarīyam* mentions the punishments of various types on the crime of stealing different items. While referring to the stealing of the goods of less expensive nature such as the theft of vegetables, firewood, grass, cot, stool, salt, water vessel (*kadava*), etc., it is stated that the penal fee of 6 *panas* would be imposed on the culprits.[24] The robbers when they were caught along with the property stolen by them should be beaten severely. If the culprit belongs to the Brahmin caste, his property should be confiscated and an imprint of the feet of a dog (*kukkachchulu*) should be stamped on the forehead of the Brahmin and be left free without being imprisoned.[25] While taking the final decision against the thieves the village headman should exhibit the wealth stolen by the thief to the villagers and in case the stolen properties hail from different villages and not from one particular village, then all the people of such villages should be summoned before declaring the final verdict of either imposing penalty or death on the culprit based on the intensity and nature of the crime.[26] When the thieves were caught for the first time with the stolen property their thumb nail should be cut, if they commit the offence for the second time and caught, his arms and legs should be cut and, if again, he commits the same offence for the third time it should not be tolerated and the culprit should be beheaded in front of all the villagers.[27] If the finest gems of gentlemen were stolen, that robber should be killed and in the case of the theft of the money of the other people, eight *panas* should be collected from them.[28] If the thieves are caught during the night time they should be punished severely by amputating their limbs and killed by piercing with sharp instruments.[29] The physical torture and the social indignities heaped on the thieves are mentioned in the work, *Yaśastilaka* of 10th century A.D. written by Sōmadēva Sūri. It is stated in connection with the episode of king Sudatta that a thief accused of robbing and murdering a barber is condemned by the judges and imposed the indignities on the thief such as riding a donkey, fastening round the neck a row of earthen vessels so that he might lose his life in 10 or 12 days.[30]

According to Pavuluru *Kaifiyat* (Guntur District) some thieves plundered the Agastyēśvara and Chennakēśavasvāmi temples of the village by breaking the doors of the temples and stealing the valuable ornaments of the gods, when the temples were not under regular worship.[31] In this connection it is also mentioned that the villagers left the place since the many lands of the Brahmins and the temples were spoiled and not properly maintained in the year A.D. 1783 when a faujdar, Sefar Jung has entrusted the administration of the area to Balladugu Venkatanarayana. It reveals that the absence of the regular worship to the gods, their maintenance and the desertion of the village had given scope for the activities of the thieves in that village. A rare epigraphical reference to the stealing of a copper plate grant by the robbers is noticed from a stone inscription from Valluru, (Bapatla Taluk) of Guntur District of the time of king Sriranga I dated in the year 1572 A.D.[32] It mentions the reissuing of the grant of 2 *puṭṭis* of land given to Bhagavatula Raṁgama of *ātrēya gōtra* by the king on the representation made to him. According to the inscription the copper plate grant issued to the donee by the same king three months before was stolen by the thieves and the matter was represented to the king. The king favourably responded to the request of the donee and at the same time has followed the procedure involved in granting the land, i.e, remeasuring the land in the presence of all the village officers and *kāryakartas* of the king and that a new stone inscription was placed at the site so that the donee will not be deprived of the possession of the land granted to him due to the stealing of the copper plates by the thieves.

Thus the close examination of the epigraphical and literary references to the heinous practice of robbery and theft reveals that the details of the professional activities of the thieves, the items stolen by them and the attitude of the people towards the thieves and the pain, suffering and misery faced by the people at the hands of the thieves, besides the role of the kings in dealing with the cases of theft in the medieval Andhra society. It also focuses on the different types of punishments imposed on the robbers when they were caught and the penal fee imposed on them depending on the nature of the crime and the caste to which the culprit belongs. Further the study brings to light how the kings ensured the safety of the possessions of the offenders, in case their properties were stolen, by re-issuing the land grants to them again. Since the work *Āmuktamālyada* was written by the Vijayanagara king Śrī Krishnadēvarāya that provides many details with regard to the behaviour and activities of the thieves, it can be assumed that the kings of the medieval times had sufficient knowledge of the cases of theft, the sufferings of the people and the punishments to be imposed on the robbers.

References

1. Mallanarya., *Rukmāngada Charitra* (*Ēkādasi Māhātmyam*), Vavilla, ed. Madras, 1924.
2. Ketana., *Vijñāneśvarīyam,* Manasa Publications, Nellore, 1989.
3. Koravi Goparaju., *Siṁhāsana Dvātriṁśaka,* 2 vols, Andhra Sahitya Parishad, Kakinada, 1933.
4. Sri Krishnadevaraya., *Āmuktamālyada,* Vavilla edition, Madras, 1930.
5. Sankra Kavi., *Hariśchandropākhyānamu,* Madras, 1924.
6. Tenali Ramakrishna., *Pāṇḍuranga Māhātmyamu,* Hyderabad, 1964.
7. Sarangu Tammayya., *Vaijayantī Vilāsamu,* Eluru.
8. Ayyalaraju Narayanamatya., *Haṁsaviṁśati,* Canto I p.37, 1. 155.
9. Dharmendrakumar Gupta., *Society and Culture in the Time of Dandin,* Delhi, 1972, p. 286.
10. Sarangu Tamayya., *op.cit.,* canto IV v. 111-113.
11. Mallana, *op.cit.,* canto III v. 32, p. 95.

12. *Ibid.*, v. 33 p. 95.
13. *Ibid.*, v. 34 p. 96.
14. Koravi Goparaju., *op.cit.*, part II, canto X, v. 118-121, p. 88.
15. Sankara kavi, *op.cit.*, canto V, v. 111-112.
16. Śrī Krishnadēvarāya., *op.cit.*, canto V, v. 80.
17. Tenali Ramakrishna., *op.cit.*, canto III, v. 52 p. 112.
18. Śrī Krishṇadēvarāya., *op.cit.*, v. 69. p. 535.
19. *Ibid.*, v. 71 p. 536-37.
20. *Ibid.*, v. 77.
21. *Ibid.*, v. 81.
22. Koravi Goparaju., *op.cit.*, v. 119-121.

    “చప్పుళ్లు లాంచుచుఁ దమ చప్పుళ్ళడఁచుచును జొచ్చి సందుల లోనం
    జొప్పడుగ కుండ నీగుచు, చెప్పులు మాటైన దాఁగుచుంచుచుఁ బురిలోన్
    ఉలుకు మ్రుగ్గునంత నొకచోట త్రుద్ధుల, యట్లు మెదలకుండ యున్నకడువు
    కొరవి యంతనంత గొదుగుచు లోపలి, మెలుకు వరసి కోటు మలుక దాట
    పాతమున్న వారపై నాల్గు జూడిద, మందు చల్లి పెద్దముగులు కొంత
    కూలఁ ద్రవ్వి రాచ కూతు రుండెడి మేడ, కత్తిరించినట్లు గంటువెట్టి”

23. Śrī Krishṇadēvarāya., *op.cit.*, v. 85.
24. Kētana., *op.cit.*, *Prāyaśchittakānda*, v. 96.
25. *Ibid.*, v. 92.
26. *Ibid.*
27. *Ibid.*, v. 99.
28. *Ibid.*, v. 99.
29. *Ibid.*
30. K.K. Handiqui., *Yaśastilaka and Indian Culture*, Sholapur. 1968, p. 125.
31. V.V. Krishna Sastry ed. *Village Kaifiyats* Part IV, *Guntur District*, Hyderabad, 1990, pp. 116-119.
32. *S.I.I.* vol. XVI No. 282.

16

ALCOHOLIC DRINKS IN MEDIEVAL ANDHRA : GLEANINGS THROUGH LITERATURE

Alcoholic drinking must have been a popular practice during the medieval times in spite of its bad effects that were realized by the people. Irrespective of their social and economic status both men and women used to enjoy the alcoholic drinks. However, some Telugu literary works of the medieval times and a few accounts left by foreigners show some distinctions among the people with regard to the types of drinks consumed by them. The existence of liquor shops, the taxes levied on the sale of liquors and the appointment of a Superintendent of liquor during the ancient times are widely well-known through Kauṭilya's *Arthaśāstra*.[1] Due to lack of adequate historical sources it often becomes difficult to ascertain whether the different types of liquors of the ancient times continued and that the Kauṭilyan administrative system of liquor control continued to the medieval times. Further, the role played by the state with regard to the control measures adopted either for the sale of liquors or for its utilization by different people during the medieval times is also not clearly known. The habit of alcoholic drinking that makes people happy and intoxicated seems to have persisted in the medieval Andhra society from the ancient times without any interruption. Studies conducted earlier on the social history of the medieval Andhra period have either totally ignored or paid less attention to this practice that has a greater impact on the behaviour and the social relations of the people. In order to understand and appreciate the social life and history of the people it is essential to know something about their interests and habits. Therefore, an attempt has been made in the present paper to highlight the social practice of alcoholic drinking, the types of liquors consumed by the people and to study its impact on the people of the society besides considering the popular perceptions and views of the people with regard to the drinking of liquors as reflected in the Telugu literary works such as *Siṁhāsana Dvātriṁsika, Śrī Kālahastī Māhātmyamu, Rukmāngada Charitra, Sudakshiṇā Pariṇayamu, Rādhā Mādhavam* and *Haṁsaviṁśati*. Further a few stone inscriptions that contained stray references to the taxes imposed on alcoholic drinks are also examined to bring out an objective and comprehensive account on the types of alcoholic drinks, its usage and impact on the medieval Andhra society.

In *Haṁsaviṁśati* of Ayyalarāju Nārāyaṇāmātya, a work of late medieval period (17th Century), it is mentioned that the art of preparation of liquor which is referred to as *mairēyamu* as one of the 64 arts of learning.[2] However, it may be mentioned that the long list of 64 arts given in an earlier work i.e., *Siṁhāsana Dvātriṁśika* that belongs to 15th century A.D. has omitted the reference to the making of alcoholic drinks, for reasons not clearly known. In the literary work *Rukmāngada Charitra* of Mallana the drinking of liquors is considered as one of the *sapta vyasanas* (seven vices) that are to be avoided by the kings.[3] While describing the bad effects of the seven vices, it is mentioned that it is because of the excessive drinking that the whole of the Yadava clan perished on this earth and, therefore, it is advisable for the kings who wish to rule the earth uninterruptedly,[4] not to involve themselves in any of the seven vices.

The type of liquors (*āsavamulu*) known to the people of the medieval times are many like those of the earlier days. Most of them were made out of flowers and fruits as their names suggest. In *Rukmāngada Charitra,* there is mention of drinks such as *śākaramu, sūnujamu, guggulu, suma ghṛritajamu, nārikēḷajamu, mādhvikamu, phalmēyamu* and *gauḍa tāḷamayamu,* etc.[5] Of these it is known that *śārkaramu* is the juice made out of sugar-cane, *guggulu* is the drink made out of gum or resin (gum guggal); *sumaghatitam* could be a type of drink made out of different scented flowers, *nārikēḷamu* is the type of drink from coconuts. *Mādhvikamu* is the type of fermented juice of grapes. The other popular varieties of liquor known from the literary works were *pushpāsava, tāḷa madhu, aikshava, madira, mairēya, kādaṁbamu, vārshamu, rati phalamu and mādhavamu,* etc.[6] It is described in them that different varieties of drinks of fine and sweet flavour were further enriched with scented smell. It appears that *tāḷa madhu* was the liquor made out of palm trees like the *nārikēḷāsava* which is made out of coconuts. Although the actual process of making liquors was not mentioned in the Telugu literary works of the period under study, it is known from an inscription of A.D. 1593 that the local chief Mahāmaṇḍalēśvara Alluḍu Raghunātharājayyadēva granted revenues realised from toddy to the temple at the rate of 2 *gadyas* per month out of *īḍiga gutta* of the village Guttipatnam amounting to 24 *gadyas* per annum.[7] It suggests that revenues on toddy were collected by the local rulers from the villages that were given on lease.

Reference has also been made to the *pānagōshṭhis,* the drinking bouts that were organized on happy occasions by the kings, nobles, officials and others where the people consumed the alcoholic drinks of different kinds in accordance with the season and individual taste. Such drinking bouts were organized at the places near the residences of prostitutes (*vēśyā vāṭikalu*) which were frequently visted by men of all classes according to *Siṁhāsana Dvātriṁśika*[8] and *Śrī Kālahastimāhātmyamu.*[9] It is also known from *Rādhā Mādhavaṁ* of Chintalapudi Ellayarya that such bouts were also organized in the inner apartments of the royal palaces and at the residences of the nobles.[10] From these works it is known that a portion of the mansion of each nobleman was set apart for celebrating the specific occasions which involve the consumption of alcoholic beverages. The *pāna gōshṭhis* were visited by the *bhogis* of both sexes and it appears that drinking liquor was treated as a special mark of refinement. The *pāna gōshthis* provided merriment to the revelrous people and sometimes it seems that liquor was taken in raw condition, but it was customary to subject it to a process of concoction by adding some ingredients to remove the strong disagreeable odour and to make it more pleasant.[11] For this purpose some devices like powdered camphor were added to remove the foul smell of spirituous liquors which were drunk. Further to sweeten the breath and to prevent belching, betel leaves and nuts were chewed. It is interesting to note that people paid great attention not only to the alcoholic drinks but also to the vessels and cups in which the drinks are served. In *Haṁsaviṁśati,* reference has been made to the *pāna pātras* as having been imported from foreign countries.[12] In *Siṁhāsana Dvātriṁśika* it is mentioned that drinks were first offered to the goddesses like Kamākshī, Mahākālī, Chaṇḍī, Kāma Jiyya, Kālī, Aṁbikā, Vindhyavāsinī, Ēkavīra and then taken by the people.[13] It may be mentioned here that *madya* is included as one in the *pañcha makaras* that are considered to be essential in the tantric rituals practised by the *sādhakas* in connection with Śākta worship. Wine, which merely intoxicates people is a good producer of a euphoric condition, in which care and anxiety are forgotten and therefore the tantric practitioners consider it a desirable drink.[14] The importance of wine in *dēvī* worship is well known from a manuscript entitled *Mahākāli-Sōdaśa-Pātra*, a collection of verses in praise of sixteen vessels filled with wine to be offered to Mahākālī.[15] *Dēvī Māhātmyamu* states that Chaṇḍikā drinks several cups of wine during her final battle with Mahishāsura. Another *Tantra* text, *Śrī Matōttara Tantra* datable to A.D. 1609 describes the yōginīs variously as swaying with the effect of wine (*madirānanda ghūrṇita*), as delighting in the pleasure of wine (*madirānanda lālasa*, *madirānanda nandita)* and as having eyes rolling through the intoxicating wine (*mada ghūrnita lōchana*)[16]. Very interestingly the *Kulārṇava Tantra* gives us an intriguing recipe for the favourite drink of the *yoginis* (*yōginī pānamutamaṁ*). According to it one part of dry ginger, two parts of lemon tree bark, three parts of black pepper corns, four parts of dhātaki(?), five blossoms, six of honey and eighty parts of jaggery are to be mixed together with water twice the quantity of honey. After twelve days of brewing it produces an enchanting liquor (*idam manōharam dravyaṁ*)[17]. The names borne by some of the yōginīs such as *Sura Priyā* (Lover of wine) and *Pisitāsavalolupā* (she, who is greedy for pressed wine) suggest their fondness for drinking wine. Siddharṣi, a Jain writer of Upamitibhāva Prapañcha Katha of 10th century A.D., refers to the worship of Chaṇḍika with wine and describes drinking bouts and merry-making in front of the shrine of the goddess with their evil consequences.[18] In the *Skanda Purāṇa*, it is stated that when a great goddess of Prabhāsakshētra killed the demons Bala, Atibala and their army, some of the demons who escaped became *kaulas* and addicted to meat, wine and women.[19] It is known from Tantras like *Kulachūḍāmani Tantra* and *Bhairava yāmala* that different meanings were given for the *pancha makaras* to suit the taste of the orthodox class and that *madya* or *madira* means milk in the case of a Brahmin; ghee or boiled butter in case of a kshatriya; honey in case of a vaiśya; liquor made from rice in case of a śūdra.[20]

From the Telugu literary works of medieval times it appears that liquor must have been very popular in those days as this social practice was well praised by the authors of the works. According to them the consumption of liquors fortifies the charm of youth through the steady use of spirituous antidotes to numerous diseases. In *Siṁhāsana Dvātriṁśika* it is stated that one lady praises the liquor as a more delicious beverage than the nectar and wonders why the divine beings had taken pains to churn the milk ocean. Further she says, "Siva drank the poison as he could not procure liquor (*vāruṇī rasam*); Chandra became thin without liquor (*sura*) and reached the head of Śiva where Ganga is securely positioned; Gaṇēśa cried in ecstasy when his belly was full and bulged with a large quantity of liquor; Shanmukha served Śakti as he was unable to drink the liquor." Likewise the merits of drinking liquor are stated in the same work in hyperbolic terms as it would give happiness and joy for all the people. In *Daśakumāra Charitra* it is stated that liquor kindles sexual desire and improves the capacity for pleasure. It draws the consciousness of sin, so counteracting morbidity. The consumption of liquor conduces to mutual confidence by removing the fetters of reticence. By repressing envy, it makes for pure joy. It encourages continual enjoyment of music and other sense impressions to gain countless and varied friendships.

The detailed descriptions given in the literary works with regard to the convivial parties reveal that they begin rather late in the night. People comprising the party squatted on the ground in a circle with the wine pots in the centre. They used to share each other's cups frequently and particularly lovers exchanged their cups probably to feel more at home in each other's company. People used to get intoxicated after drinking the liquors and as a result they lost their balance and behaved differently with each other. They laughed loudly, found it difficult to speak properly. They spoke incoherently without minding their actual relations with each other with words stammered quite often. They faltered in addressing each others and at times lost their balance totally. They slapped each other and uttered words and phrases causing delight to their lovers. Some people were even unmindful of their dress and went about naked. It may be mentioned here that all the descriptions contained in the Telugu works discussed above are all suggestive of the consumption of liquors of different types in medieval times and that the praise showered on liquor as excelling the nectar and such other terms were not mere theory. On the other hand, it is observed that all the religious texts like *Manusmriti* had forbidden the consumption of *Sura* for the three higher classes—Brahmins, Kshatriyas and Vaisyas. Drinking by a Brahmin was considered a great sin (*mahā pātaka*) in *Manu Smriti*.[21] In case of any indulgence by a Brahmin in drink the expiatory rite imposed on such persons is none other than death. Such statements given in the Hindu religious texts of the earlier period with regard to the taboo imposed on drinking and also the different expiatory rites indicate a particular value system during the ancient times. However, during the medieval times, the spirituous liquors do not seem to have been completely avoided in spite of the fact that the Gentile and Muhammaden law prohibited the use of wine equally, as it has been observed by Bernier and others in their accounts.[22] According to Bernier the liquor peculiar to India is arac, a spirit drawn by distillation from unrefined sugar.[23] The other most common drink was tary or toddy, which has been referred to by practically all the foreign travellers who visited India.

The literary references of the medieval times examined above reveal that theoretically drinking sprituous liquors was considered a vice and social sin and its consumption was condemned as it clouds the reason and deprives it of its powers. However, several references in them praise its taste, smell, and the delight it gives to those who consume it prove that the drinking of liquor was quite popular and common among men and women during the medieval times in Andhra region. Probably it must have been the excessive drinking that was condemned, for it would deprive the people of their senses. Since the revenues collected on the intoxicating liquors such as toddy formed an important source of revenue to the state during the medieval times it may be said that drinking liquor continued to be popular in medieval times in spite of its bad effects on the senses and the behaviour of the people.

References

1. *Arthaśāstra* of Kautilya, ed. by R. Shamastri., Mysore, 8th edition, 1967, ch. XXV pp. 133-137.
2. *Haṁsaviṁśati* of Ayyalaraju Nārāyaṇāmātyas, Madras, 1964 canto I line 155, p. 37.
3. *Rukmāngada Charitra* of Mallana, Madras, 1924 Canto III, v. 76 p. 104.
4. *Ibid.*
5. *Ibid.*, canto III, v. 227 p. 137.
6. *Siṁhāsana Dvātriṁśika* of Koravi Goparaju, Kakinada, 1933, Canto I v. 256, p. 103.
7. S.I.I. vol. XVI, No. 304.
8. *Siṁhāsana Dvātriṁśika., op.cit.*, p. 103.
9. *Śrī Kālahastī Māhātmyamu* of Dhurajati, Madras, 1914, p. 49-50.
10. *Rādhā Mādhavam* of Chintalapudi Ellayary, Canto IV.
11. N. Venkataramanayya., *Studies in the History of the Third Dynasty of Vijayanagara Empire,* Madras, 1935, p. 390.
12. *Haṁsaviṁśati., op.cit.*, Canto V. 353, p. 378.
13. *Siṁhāsana Dvātriṁśika., op.cit.*, Canto V. 259, p. 103.
14. Sudhaka Chattopadhyaya., *Reflections on the Tantras,* Delhi, 1978, p. 25.
15. *Manuscript No. 858/B.D. 189,* Asiatic Society, Bombay; Vidya Dehejiya., *Yogini culto and Temples : A Tantric Tradition.*, Delhi, 1986, p. 57.
16. Śrī Matōttara Tantra ed. by Janadhan andya, 1976, ch. 20. v. 35, 113, 127, 197.
17. V. Taranath and Arthur Avalon., ed. *Kaulāṇava Tantra* ch. 5, v. 21-23.
18. K.K. Hand., *Yaśastlaka and Indan Culture,* Sholapur, 1968, p. 395.
19. *Ibid.*, p. 355; *Skandapurāṇa,* chapter 119 of *Pabhasakshtra Mahatmya.*
20. *Ibid.*, Also see T.N. Mishra., *Impact of Tantra on Religion and Art,* Delhi, 1997, p. 38.
21. *Manu Smṛiti,* chapter XI, v. 54.
22. Craufurd., *Sketches Chiefly Related to the History, Religion, Learning and Manners of Hindus,* London, 1790, p. 281.
23. Bernier., Francois: *Travels in the Mughal Empire,* Oxford, 1934, p. 252.

17

Historical Insights into Vegetation and Wild Life:

Reconstruction Through Inscriptions and Literature (17th & 18th Centuries A.D.)

The careful management of water resources, the productive use of land by the people, the interest evinced by the rulers and state administration give rise to the beautiful landscape of Andhra region during the pre-colonial period. Particularly the Qutb Shahis and their successors have initiated the horticultural plots and enclosed orchards in the Golconda State that reveal Persian influence. With water brought with great difficulty and extraordinary engineering skill, from the mountains to the dry plains by underground and surface canals and storing rainwater in well-constructed tanks and reservoirs for its usage in dry season, the rulers of the day have contributed much to the growth and development of garden lands. There are thematic connections that link the spatial and aesthetic qualities of these arrangements of land, water and vegetation. The art of gardening had become a science and laying out gardens was an indispensable feature in the temples and town planning in ancient times. It is these sensibilities, which were reflected in their gardens and referred to in the inscriptions of

Andhra as *vāṭikās, nandanavanams, tōpus, pushpavanams* and *āramas,* which reveal a very refined art of gardening. The cultural study of any region or period will not be completed without considering the main factors of the environment that include—air, water, soil, climate, flora and fauna, etc., and its interaction with the human activities. To bring out the comprehensive history of the human societies of any region and period fruitfully, it is needed to view it from an ecological perspective. Historical studies with ecological perspectives are highly useful in reconstructing the economic geography, India's maritime trade with foreign countries as well as the inland trade and commerce since India's trade with Europe had increased during the 17th century. A number of European merchants and travellers had visited the country and left detailed accounts of the country. Their observations about the regions and areas they passed through are of immense value to know about the natural environment that existed in Andhra during 17th & 18th centuries A.D. It is attempted to reconstruct the activities of the Andhra in relation to the taming of certain species of plants and animals as referred to in the historical sources and to present the then natural environment that existed, particularly the vegetation and animal life for a better understanding of the human adaptations to it which brings about changes in the history of the culture of the people. For this purpose the stray references contained in the inscriptions and Telugu literature are taken up as the major sources of study on the subject besides the account of foreign travellers. On the other hand some of the paintings of the Qutb Shahi rulers also display the beautiful gardens, the tamed animals and wild life in accordance with the themes of the paintings in a very colourful and picturesque manner.

The maps prepared for the Mughal era by Irfan Habib and Shireen Moosvi provide an idea about the forest, scrub and desert areas in India as they are based on the descriptive information given in the historical sources for the Mughal period. The vegetation maps of 16th-17th centuries A.D. show the large size of forested area and waste land set against the much more restricted area of the agricultural zone at the time.[1] Although it is difficult to know many of the details of the agricultural, forest, scrub and desert zones through them about the Andhra region since they have not incorporated the details of the agricultural clearings within the main block of the forest, they are useful while comparing them with the authoritative maps of vegetation features valid for 1909. It shows the change that has taken place during the last four hundred years and reveals the impact of technology, industry, trade and human activity in the disappearance of the forest cover and changes in the course of river systems and their drainage pattern.

The existence of forest cover in the Deccan plateau extending from the Krishna-Tungabhadra confluence almost to the delta, south of the river Krishna and also existing in patches on its left bank can be noticed from the map. Probably because of this forest cover the presence of elephants in the Eastern Deccan can be noticed from the historical sources of the earlier centuries. The offices of the State administration such as *Gaja Sāhiṇi* and *Aśva Sāhiṇi* appointed to look after the elephant and horse forces and the popular reference to the rulers of Kalinga region, as Gajapatis are sufficient indicators of the existence of elephants in good number. Further, from the writings of Tavernier that wild elephants were caught just north of Tirupati,[2] it can be suggested that the great block of forest cover extend into southern Andhra. Not only from the ecological point of view but also as an economic factor the existence of the forests is considered as very important. People had realized the value of timber for its use in the construction of their dwellings, public institutions and for various other activities such as shipbuilding. In the Anonymous Relation it is mentioned that the timber for shipbuilding was brought down from higher up the river.[3] It is presumed that teak that grows abundantly along the course of river Godavari is floated down the river.[4] In *Haṁsaviṁsati,* reference has been made to deer, black buck, wild cat, mongoose, lions, hunting dogs, English dogs and monkeys as the items brought to his homeland by the merchant Vishṇu Dāsa through his sea borne trade.[5] The Anonymous Relations mention a long list of many kinds of animals including the tame and wild animals. It is stated that tigers, elephants, bears, leopards, civet cats and monkeys were in abundance.[6] Reference has been made to the spotted deer (*cervus axis*) with its body covered by many white spots and horns. Besides these another kind of deer i.e, the Indian antelope or black buck (*Antelope cervicapra*) without any spots have the horns erect and twisted like a screw, very smooth and very handsome in appearance were tamed when found while they are very young. These animals used to follow the person anywhere, when tamed and come to eat at table or out of the hand. It is reported that foxes are found in great abundance and snakes in enormous numbers and of them some are very poisonous and that a person will die on the spot if he is bitten by such snakes. Another variety of snakes called hooded snakes *cobra toppella* is also considered very poisonous and is found in great numbers. A kind of animal called elk (most probably the same as Sambar) many strange beasts, a kind of field rat, which is reddish in colour and extremely good at eating and several animals that are tamed during this period are mentioned in his account. The list of tamed animals includes oxen, cows, buffaloes, sheep and goats of three varieties, which do not yield much milk. Horses were also tamed and it is mentioned that all the horses of the country are of small size, which are better for travelling. The large horses used for military work were imported from Petane, Arabia and Ormuz. The detailed list of wild and domestic animals furnished by the anonymous author closely corroborates with the information that can be gathered from the indigenous literary sources. The hunting dogs (*vēṭa jāgilālu* or *vēṭa vēpulu*) useful for hunting the wild animals used to accompany their masters while they go for hunting and is referred to in many Telugu literary works of the period.[7] It is known from them that these dogs which are of different types can be distinguished by their speed, alacrity, colour, size, and physical appearance were tamed well specifically for the purpose of finding out the traces of the wild animal while proceeding to hunt them. It is interesting to note that their masters who christened them with the names that reflect their qualities and physical features tamed these hunting dogs affectionately.[8] While describing the hunting activities of prince Sudyumna, Kanuparti Abbayamatya explained the best qualities of the hunting dogs in a very detailed manner in his Telugu literary work *Kavirājamanōranjanam* (of A.D. 1750). It is stated that the dogs namely *Bebbuli, Tupāki, Suḍigāli, Piḍugu Tunaka, Bhūtanātha, Dāḍipōtu, Gaṁḍa Goḍḍali and Doṁgala Miṁḍagīdu* walked in front of the team of the hunters and the prince while their remarkable achievement like killing the lions, chasing the deers and antelopes and capturing them and attacking the wild animals like *Kommu Pandi* and *Nala Pandi* were explained to the Prince by his fellow hunters.[9] The cocks were the most familiar domestic birds and cock-fighting was one of the popular pastime activities of the people. Like the dogs tamed and named by the people for hunting as well as for security reasons, the cocks were also tamed and named for the purpose of cock fighting. In *Śrī Kuvalayāśva Charitrmu* Savaram China Nārāyaṇa Kavi of 17th century A.D. mentioned the names of cocks as Gauḍa, Maila, Salāyattu and Kāki vanne before describing in detail the course of events of cock fighting.[10] A similar type of description about cock-fighting and the long list of names of the cocks were furnished in *Haṁsaviṁśati*. With regard to the list of different animals tamed by the people of *Golla* caste, Narayanamatya provides some useful information in his work. While referring to the wealth of a famous person of the *Golla* community namely Vijaya, it is mentioned that he possessed several flocks of sheep of different names like *Kurupavi, Dōra, Chāra, Nalagoṇḍa, Eragoṇḍa, Mūja, Bollivi, Narigivi, Nettu, Jōḍu, Pula, Nallavi, Eṛravi, Barigīvi, Moṛrivi, Geraka, Pallavi, Pullavi and Chillavi*.[11] The names given to the sheep mentioned above reveals that they were named according to their physical features and colour. Further a list of the names of goats that includes *Bōḷa, Poḍa, Maṭṭe, Bolli, Puri, Jala, Vala, Pulla, Erbatta, Chāra Baragi, Karaku Geḍḍamu, Teli Maṭṭe, Chēmaṭṭe, Kāre, Passe, Maila, Batta, Koratala, Pūja, Kapila, Kanne, Boli Chukka, Pallavi, Morri, Gavara* and *Dora* is given which once again demonstrates that their names were given on the basis of their colour, age, physical appearance including their deformities. The other animals found at the home of the shepherd were she-buffaloes (*enumulu*) and the he-buffaloes, mares (*gōḍigalu*) and rams. Besides these tamed animals which were considered as highly useful from the economic point of view as well as for the upkeep of the ecological balance of the human environment in his rural and agrarian setting, information is forthcoming from the same literary work, *Haṁsaviṁśati* in a different context. While describing the themes of the paintings done by Chitraghana, the author of the work gave a long list of animals and birds whose pictures were drawn in colours. The list of animals include lion, elephant, deer, rhinoceros, pig, tiger, wild bull, *chamara,* a type of sheep, *Gavaya* (*Gurupōtu*), bear, big antelope, rabbit, fox, ass, ram, dog, cat, monkey, mongoose, chameleon, spider, rat, snake, crocodile, goat, fish, tortoise, oyster, scorpion, leach, cow, bull frog, squirrel, baboon, etc. A long list of birds which depend for their livelihood on the small insects, fish, worms, flesh and vegetable matter of different categories is given in the same work. A distinction has been made in the species of birds on the basis of their habitat, food habits, the predator-prey relationship, their ecological setting, physiology and anatomy. It refers to the type of birds ranging from scavenger birds and vultures to that of a variety of small birds who could devour snakes to that of a variety of small birds like the sparrows of different varieties such as *Bōlaḍu, Pichchuka, Bangāru Pichchuka*. A wide variety of bird species that could be categorized under eight broad groups and known by their popular names based on their physical features are mentioned in the work. The list of birds given below (Table 1) as mentioned in the work *Haṁsaviṁśati* provides an idea about the existence of the different types of birds and the kind of ecological setting that prevailed in Āndhradēśa during 17th century A.D.

The above table reveals the existence of different species of birds besides their habitat, the specific activities by which they were known and the variety of birds through the distinction in colour, size and shape. Although the list is not exhaustive it presents a detailed account of the wide variety of birds.

Laying out gardens and digging wells to water the flowering plants is quite often referred to in the inscriptions and literature of the period. Particularly, for the purpose of providing flowers for the ritual service in the temples, people used to make liberal donations to the temples. Although the details of the varieties of flowers grown in the temple gardens is not known from the inscriptions, *Haṁsaviṁśati* provides a detailed description of the varieties of scented, colourful and attractive flower plants and trees grown in the temple garden that are useful for offering to the gods. It refers to the varieties of jasmines, *saṁpenga*, *jājulu*, *Gannēru*, *Virajāji*, sunflowers, *ponnelu*, *pārijātamulu*, *chēmanti*, lotus flowers *sūryakānt*, *tāmaras*, *pogaḍas*, *turāyi*, grass flowers, *māchapatri*, *gaggera*, *maruvamu*, *kuruvēru*, *davanamu*, *vaṭṭivērus*, and *bilva* trees. Besides the flower gardens a good deal of information can be gathered about the different types of agricultural crops grown during this period. As many as 113 varieties of rice are mentioned in *Haṁsaviṁśati,* which are distinctly named after the size, quality, colour, shape and smell.

The inscriptional references of the Qutb Shahi period, reveal the concern of the rulers and the officials for laying the gardens and granting them to the temples. An inscription dated A.D. 1670 refers to the gift of a fruit garden of bananas planted on the tank bund in Kuvvam to Tervikkōlēśvarasvāmi in the reign of Abdullah Qutb Shah.[12] Another record from Lepakshi, Anantapur district dated A.D. 1672 refers to the garden lands of coconut plantations (*Tenkāya thōṭa*).[13] It is noticed from an inscription dated A.D. 1536 of Moyiḷḷa Kāluva that the garden lands were granted on the occasion of *Daśami Mahōtsav* to lord Tiruvengalanātha.[14] In this context it is mentioned that the garden contains the trees like coconut, mango, jackfruit, *amla, velaga,* tamarind and black jamun. Besides the granting of fruit-bearing trees and gardens, people showed interest in laying gardens of flowering plants and digging wells. The laying down of gardens usually goes hand in hand with the practice of granting the tanks or wells to the temples as water is essential for the growth and sustenance of the gardens. Several references are found in the inscriptional literature, wherein deliberate attempts were made during the medieval period to encourage and inspire the people to contribute liberally for the granting of a tank, well or digging up of canal for providing water resources by treating such acts as one of the seven meritorious acts, i.e., *saptasaṁtānas*. On the other hand, rarely, we could gain some information with regard to the acts of dissuading the people not to indulge in any acts of spoiling by defecation in the water of the rivers, tanks, gardens, temple premises, caves and places where the *kuśa* grass grows. While referring to the results and punishments meted out by the culprits in hell after death it is stated that a person who spoils the water resources cannot move hither and thither without spilling his brains from the head.[15]

The concern of the people in the Andhra society for environmental protection and wild life preservation are very well reflected in the Telugu literature of the period. For the purpose of encouraging afforestation and to discourage the felling down of trees that would cause soil erosion and changes in the weather conditions, it was observed that people who were responsible for the acts such as cutting down trees were treated as the culprits and cutting or felling down of fruit bearing trees was treated as a crime of serious nature. In *Nāsikētōpākhyānamu* Daggupalli Duggana mentioned that the persons who felled down the trees with the axe will meet the

Table 1: List of Birds mentioned in *Haṁsaviṁśati*

Hawk	Pigeon	Sparrow	Hen	Owl	Crane	Other varieties	Birds known by specific activity
1	**2**	**3**	**4**	**5**	**6**	**7**	**8**
Oraṇamu	*Kuki*	*Kāṭukapiṭṭa*	*Chādela Kōḍi*	*Gabbulgu*	*Ādelu*	*Aṁbati Jōrigāḍu*	*Ēṭrinta*
Kaṇuju	*Guvva*	*Koṇḍa*	*Cheruvu Kōdi*	*Gubbiligāḍu*	*Kakkera*	*Ullangi*	*Kankaṇamu*
		Pichchuka					
Giddu	*Nela*	*Gaḍḍi Piṭṭa*	*Nīru Kōḍi*	*Ḍabbu*	*Kannelēḍi*	*Ēkula Nārigāḍu*	*Kanubanti*
Jalakaṭṭe	*Pallati*	*Pasirika Piṭṭa*	*Bolli Kōḍi*		*Gūḍa bātu*	*Kalledu*	*Kauju*
Jāvaḷamu	*Penuguvva*	*Pasupumudda*	*Mutte Kōḍi*		*Tella Kokkera*	*Kaluku*	*Gijigāḍu*
Bairi	*Bakadari*	*Pikilipiṭṭa*	*Munugu Kōḍi*		*Pedda Kokkera*	*Kukuru*	*Chīkurāyi*
					Guṁḍaṁgi		
Vārvamu	*Beḷava*	*Pōtapiṭṭa*			*Kērajamu*	*Jittaṁgi*	
Gūba	*Lakōri*	*Bangāru*			*Kaiju*	*Jibbidāyi*	
		Pichchuka					
Vēsaḍamu	*Pāvurāyi*					*Gunnaṁgi*	*Tītuvu*
Sālvamu	*Kūkilu*					*Goṁgaḍi*	*Palavariṁta*
Gaṇḍabhēruṇḍa	*Oḍḍilu*					*Jīnuva*	*Pāmula*
							Mringuḍu

1	2	3	4	5	6	7	8
Garuḍa	*Pallatilu*					*Daba*	*Pennada*
							Pulgu
Dēga	Battigāṁḍru					*Nalla kappeta*	*Paiḍi Kaṁṭi*
Saṁpati gradda						*Nāmāla Kētadu*	*Bārātamu*
Rabandu						*Pagaḍapu jitta*	*Meela*
							Mrichchu
						Paṭṭu Jīnuvū	*Mrānipōtu pulugu*
						Pūrēḍu	*Lakumuki*
						Pedise	*Vana Koyila*
						Pōḍipiṭṭā	*Vennela pulugu*
						Pōnupenṭi	*Mālakāki*
						Pannaṁgī	*Kērajamulu*
						Pōtapiṭṭa	
						Pōladu	
						Munuga Pūjitta	
						Mūga	
						Lavukapiṭṭa	
						Mūga	
						Lavukapiṭṭa	
						Vaṁgapaṇḍu	
						Vājamu	
						Veliche	
						Sivaḍu	

same punishment and he will be cut down with the axe in the hell after his death. A person who spoils the agricultural fields that belongs to others will be subjected to fire.[16] Further it is also mentioned that killing the animals like cat, bull and calf was viewed very seriously and it is stated that such persons would be born in their future like tiger and sheep.

Thus the above study discloses that the people have considered the act of preservation and protection of vegetation and animals as not only socially useful and productive but also treated them as bringing merit to them in their future life after death. The popular beliefs, customs and faiths of the people that revolve around the worship of the elements of nature, certain trees and animals that are recorded in the literary works of the period, demonstrate the awareness of the people for environmental protection and preservation. Although the information is scanty and limited in its nature, a careful examination of the historical sources with a view to understand the response of the people and their approach to deal with the issues related to the environment has thus provided some historical insights with regard to the growing of orchards, gardens, fruit and flower gardens and temple gardens with a variety plants and trees, besides throwing a welcome light on the existence of a wide variety of animals, the practice of taming certain animals for purposes of hunting, milching and past time activities.

References

1. Shireen Moosvi., "Man and Nature in Mughal Era," *Symposium Papers: 5, Indian History Congress,* 54th Session, Delhi, 1993.
2. Jean Baptist Tavernier., *Travel in India* I, tr. V Bali, ed. W. Crooke, London, 1925 pp. 273-275.
3. Moreland., *Relations of Golconda of Early Seventeenth Century,* p. 80.
4. *Godavari District Manual,* 67.
5. Ayyalaaju Narayanamatya., *Haṁsaviṁśati,* Madras, 1964 Canto V, v. 354, p. 379.
6. Moreland., *op.cit.,* p. 85.

7. *Hariśchndrōpākhyānamu* of Sankara kvi (16th century A.D.), *Chandrabhānu Charitramu* of Tarigonda Mallana (16th century A.D.) and *Haṁsaviṁśati* of Ayyalaraju Narayanamatya (17th Century A.D.), *Kavirāja Manōranjanam* of Kanuparti Abbayamatya (18th century A.D.).
8. M. Krishna Kumari., *Facets of Andhra Culture,* Delhi 1999, pp. 177-185.
9. Kanuparti Abbayamatya., *Kavirāja Manōranjanam,* Madras, 1929, v. 82-96, pp. 41-42.
10. Savaram China Narayana kavi., *Śrī Kuvalayāśva Charitramu,* Kakinaa, 1904, Canto IV v. 206.
11. *Haṁsaviṁśati,* canto II, v. 76-79, p. 85.
12. *S.I.I.* vol. X no. 763.
13. *Ibid.*, no. 766.
14. *Inscriptions of Cuddapah District* vol. II, no. 124.
15. *Rukmangada Charitra*, canto II, v. 39.

    నదులలోఁ దటాకముల వనంబులందు దేవతా
    సదన కూప గోష్ఠ బిల కుశ స్థలంబులందు దు
    ర్గదముననే మలంబు విడిన మానుషాధముల భయం
    బొందవేఁ గదలఁ దలల మెదడు లాలుక నడవ వేదాగ్నిఁ.

16. *Nāsikētōpākhyānamu*, v. 87 p. 120.

BIBLIOGRAPHY

Epigraphical Sources

A Collection of the Inscriptions on Copper plates and stones in the Nellore District, 3 Volumes, Reprint, Delhi, 1990.

A Topographical List of the Inscriptions in the Madras Presidency, 3 Vols. Ed. by V. Rangacharya (Madras, 1919).

Annual Reports on Epigraphy, 1967, 1977

Annual Reports on Indian Epigraphy.

Annual Reports on the Mysore Archaeological Department, Bangalore, 1906-39; Mysore and Hyderabad, 1965

Annual Reports on South Indian Epigraphy, Madras, 1887-1945.

Copper Plate Inscriptions in the Hyderabad Museum, Vol. 1, Ed. by N. Ramesan (Hyderabad, 1962).

Copper Plate Inscriptions of Andhra Pradesh State Museum, Vol. 11, Ed. by N. Ramesan (Hyderabad, 1970).

Early Telugu Inscriptions Up to 1100 A.D. by B. Radha Krishna, Hyderabad, 1971

Epigraphia Andhrica.

Epigraphia Carnatica.

Epigraphia Indica.

Historical Inscriptions of Southern India and Outlines of Political History, Ed. by Robert Sewell, Madras, 1932.

Hyderabad Archaeological Series.

Indian Antiquary.

Inscriptions of Andhradesa, M. Rama Rao.

Inscriptions of Andhra Pradesh, Cuddapah District, Hyderabad, Vols. 3.

Journal of Andhra Historical Research Society.
Journal of Andhra History and Culture.
Journal of Epigraphical Society of India.
Sasana Padya Manjari, (Telugu,), Ed. by J. Ramayya Pantulu.
Sasana Samputi, (Telugu), B.N. Sastry, Hyderabad, 1973.
Select Stone Inscriptions of Andhra Pradesh, Ed. by P.B. Desai, Hyderabad, 1962.
South Indian Inscriptions.
Temple Inscriptions of Andhra Pradesh, Srikakulam District, Ed. by N. Ramesan and Mukunda Rao, Hyderabad.

Literary Sources

Aniruddha Charitramu of Abbayāmatya, Vavilla ed., Madras, 1924.
Arthaśāstra of Kautilya Tr. by R. Shamsastry, Mysore, 1967.
Chandrabhānu Charitramu of Tarigoppulu Mallana, Andhra Sahitya Parishad, Madras, 1922.
Chokkanatha Charitra by Pachchakappurapu Tiruvengalraju, ed. by T. Chandrasekharan, Madras, 195.
Dasakumara Charitra of Dandin, Tr. by Ketana, Vavilla ed., Madras, 1925.
Haṁsaviṁśati of Ayyalraju Narayanamtya, Vavilla ed., Madras, 1964.
Hariśchandrōpākhyānamu of Sankara Kavi, Vavilla ed., Madras, 1924.
Jaiminībhāratamu of Pillallamarri Pina Virabhadra Kavi, Madras, 1958.
Kukkutēśvara Śatakam of Kuchimanchi Timma Kavi, Vavilla ed., Madras 1919.
Nāsikētōpākhyānamu, A.P. Sahitya Academy, Hyderabad, 1977.
Nīlāsundarī Pariṇayamu of Kuchimanchi Timmakavi, Vavilla ed., Madras, 1948.
Nītisīsapadyaśatakamu of Tallapaka Peda Tirumalarya, Andhra Sahitya Parishad, Madras, 1917.
Pāṇḍurangamāhātmyamu of Tenali Rama Krishna Kavi.
Rāghavābhyudayam of Chintalapalli Chayapati ed. by B.Ramaraju, A.P. Sahitya Academy, Hyderabad.
Rāmalingēśvara Śatakarnu of Adidarn Surakavi, Vavilla ed. Madras, 1923.
Rukmāngada Charitra of Praudhakavi Mallana, Vavilla edition, Madras, 1924.
Śakuntala Parinayamu of Peddada Nagarajaṛnatya, K.R. Venkata Krishna Rao, Madras, 1900.

Śakuntala Pariṇayamu of Pilamarri Pina Virabhadra Kavi, Vavilla ed., Madras, 1923.

Sāmbōpākhyānamu of Ramaraju Rangappa Kavi, Kakinada 1932.

Sānandōpakhyānamu of Kota Sivarama Kavi.

Śataka Samuchchayamu, 2 Parts, Andhra Sahitya Parishad, Kakinada, 1933.

Siṁhāsana Dvātrimsika of Koravi Goparaju, 2 Vols. Andhra Sahitya Parishad, Kakinada, 1933.

Śrī Kuvalayāśva Charitramu of Savaram China Narayana Nayaka, Kakinada, 1904.

Śrī Vēnkaṭāchala Māhātmyamu of Tarigonda Venkam Adiba, Vavilla ed., Madras, 1914.

Śuksaptati of Palavekari Kadiripati, Vavilla ed., Madras, 1951.

Vaijayantī Vilasamu of Sarangu Tammaya, Nandiraju Chalapati Rao, Eluru.

Vikramārka Charitramu of Jakkana, Andhra Pradesh Sahitya Academy, Hyderabad, 1968.

Vīrabhadra Vijayamu of Bammera Potana, Vavilla ed., Madras, 1952.

Visvaguṇādarśamu of Venkatdhvari Tr. by Ramakrishna Kavulu, Madras, 1917.

Yayāti Charitramu of Ponnikanti Telaganarya, Vavilla ed., Madras, 1956.

Secondary Sources

Agrawala, V.S., *The Heritage of Indian Art,* Delhi, 1984.

Altekar, A.S., *The Position of Women in Hindu Civilization,* Banaras, 1938.

Amritanandanatha, *Śrī Chakra Pūja,* Devipuram, 2001.

Appadorai, A., *Economic Conditions of Southern India A.D. 1000-1500,* Madras, 1936.

Appa Rao, V. (Ed.), *Reddi Samchika,* Rajahmundry, 1947.

Arasaratnam, S., *Masulipatnam and Cambay; A History of Two Port Towns,* Delhi, 1994.

———, *Merchants, Companies and Commerce on the Coromandel Coast A.D. 1650-1740,* Delhi, 1986.

———, *Maritime Trade in Seventeenth Century,* Delhi, 1994.

Banerjea., J.N., *Development of Hindu Iconography,* 2nd revised ed., Calcutta, 1956.

Barry Reay, (Ed.), *Popular Culture in Early Modern England,* London, 1985.

Baudhayana *Dharma Sūtras,* Trans, by George Buhler, Sacred Book of the East, Series, Vol. XIV.

Bernier, Francois, *Travels in the Mughal Empire,* Oxford, 1934.

Beuard, E., *Chinnamastā, The Awful Buddhist and Hindu Tantric Goddess,* Buddhist Tradition Series, Vol. 22, Delhi, 1994.

Bhagawant Sahai, *Iconography of Minor Hindu and Buddhist Deities,* Delhi, 1975.

Bhandarkar, R.G., *Vaishnavism, Saivism and Minor Religious Systems,* Strasbourg, 1931.

Bhattacharya, N.N., *History of the Tantric Religion : An Historical Ritualistic and Philosophical Study,* 2nd revised ed., Delhi, 1999.

Bhattasali, N.K., *Iconography of Buddhist and Brahmanical Sculptures in the Dacca Museum,* 1929.

Biardeau, Madeleine, *Hinduism: Anthropology of a Civilization,* Delhi, 1989.

Bigsby, C.W.E. (Ed.), *Approaches to Popular Culture,* London, 1976.

Blackburn, Stuart H., "Death and Deification: Folk Cults in Hinduism", History of Religions 24, 3:255-74, 1985.

Blackburn, Stuart H. and Ramanujan, A.K., *Another Harmony: New Essays on the Folklore of India*, Berkeley, 1986.

Bose, D.N., *Tantras: Their Philosophy and Occult Secrets,* Calcutta, 3rd ed., 1956.

Brijesh Krishna, *The Art under Gurjara Pratiharas,* Delhi, 1984.

Carman, John B and Frederique A Margin, Ed., *Purity and Auspiciousness in Indian Society,* Leiden, 1985.

Carstairs G Morris, *The Twice Born: A Study of a Community of High Caste Hindus,* Bloomington, 1967.

Chattopadhyaya, Sudhakar, *Reflelctions on the Tantras,* Delhi, 1978.

Chintamani Chakravarty, *The Tantra Studies on Their Religion and Literature,* Calcutta, 1963.

Claudine, Bautze - Picron, CNRS., Ed., *Makaranda: Essays in Honour of D.P. James C Harle,* Delhi, 1990.

Clothey Fred W. (ed.), *Images of Man: Religion and Historical Process in South Asia,* Madras, 1982.

Cohn Bernard, S., *An Anthropologist Among the Historians and other Essays, Delhi*, 1990.

Craufurd, *Sketches Chiefly Related to the History, Religion, Learning and Manners of Hindus,* London, 1790.

Das, H.C., *Tantricism - A Study of the Yogini Cult,* Delhi, 1981.

Das, R.M., *Women in Manu and His Seven Commentators,* Varanasi, 1962.

Dehejea, Vidya, *Early Stone Temples of Orissa,* Delhi, 1979.

———, *Jogini Cult and Temples: A Tantric Tradition,* Delhi, 1986.

De Josselin de Jong, P.E., *Structural Anthropology in the Netherlands,* The Hagues, 1977.

Dhruvarajan V., *Hindu Women and Power of Ideology*, Delhi, 1989.

Dirks, Nicholas, B., *The Hollow Crown: Ethnohistory of an Indian Kingdom,* Cambridge, 1987.

Donaldson, Thomas E., *Hindu Temple: Art of Orissa,* Leiden, 1986.

Dubois, Abbe, *Hindu Manners, Customs and Ceremonies,* Oxford, 1897.

Dundes, Alan, *The Study of Folklore,* New Jersey, 1965.

Dwivedi R.C. (ed.), *Contribution of Jainism to Indian Culture,* Patna, 1975.

Eschmann A., Kulke H and Tripathi C.C. (ed.), *The Cult of Jagannath and Regional Traditions of Orissai,* Delhi, 1978.

Frazer, *Golden Bough,* London, 1900.

Freud, Sigmund, *An Outline of Psycho Analysis,* 1940.

———, *The Interpretation of Dreams,* Trans. and ed. By James Strachey, New York, 1961.

Fuller, C.J., *The Camphor Flame Popular Hinduism and Society in India,* Princeton University Press, Viking, Delhi, 1992.

———, *Servants of the Goddesses: The Priests of a South Indian Temples,* Delhi, 1991.

Fuller C.J., "Royal Divinity and Human Kingship in the Festivals of a South Indian Temple", *South Asian Social Scientist*-1 : 3-45, 1985.

Galey, Jean-Claude., "Reconsidering Kingship in India: An Ethnological Perspective", *History and Anthropology,* 4: 123-87, 1989.

Gangadharam, N., *Minneru,* Rajahmundry, 1968.

Gardiner, Juliet (ed.), *What is History Today?* London, 1988.

Gautama, *Dharma Sutra-Sacred Laws of the Aryas,* Trans. by George Buhler (SBE Series, Vol. II).

Getty, Alice., *Ganesa: A Monograph on the Elephant Faced God,* Oxford, 1936.

Goldman, Robert, P., "Fathers, Sons and Gurus: Oedipal Conflict in the Sanskrit Epics", Journal of Indian Philosophy, 6: 325-92.

———, *Gods, Priests and Warriors: The Bhrugus of the Mahābhārata,* New York, 1977.

Gopala Krishna Murty, S., *Jain Vestiges in Andhra,* Hyderabad, 1963.

Gopinatha Rao, T.A., *Elements of Hindu Iconography,* 2 Vols., 2nd edn., Delhi, 1971.

Gertrude, Himmalfarb., *The New History and the Old,* Cambridge, 1987.

Ghosh, A. (ed.), *Jaina Art and Architecture,* Delhi, 1975.

Ghoshal, U.N., *A History of Hindu Political Theories from the Earliest Times to the End of Seventeenth,* Calcutta, 1923, 2nd ed., 1927.

Gudrun, Buhnemann, *Forms of Gaṇēśa: A Study Based on the Vidyāṇavatantra,* Wichtrach, 1989.

Gupta, Dharmendra Kumar, *Society and Culture in the Time of Dandin,* Delhi, 1972.

Gupta, D.K., *Society and Culture in the Time of Dandin,* Delhi, 1972.

Hall, Kenneth R., *Structure and Society in Early South India: Essays* in Honour of Noboru Karashima, Delhi, 2001.

Handa, Devendra (ed.), *Indological Studies,* Delhi, 1987.

Haudelman, Don and David Shulman, *God Inside Out: Siva's Game of Dice,* New York, 1997.

Handiqui, K.K., *Yaśastilaka and Indian Culture,* Sholapur, 1968.

Hans, Bakker (ed.), *The Sacred Centre as the Focus of Political Interest,* Groningen, 1992.

Haripriya, Rangarajan., *Varaha Images in Madhya Pradesh: An Iconographical Study,* Delhi, 1997.

———, *Spread of Vaishnavism in Gujarat up to 1600 A.D.*, Delhi, 1990.

———, (ed.), *Jainism - Art, Architecture, Literature and Philosophy,* Delhi, 2001.

Harle, J.C. and Andrew, Topsfield, *Indian Art in Ashmolean Museum,* Oxford, 1987.

Harman, William P., *The Sacred Marriage of a Hindu Goddess,* Bloomington, 1989.

Heesterman, J.C., *The Inner Conflict of Tradition: Essays in Indian Ritual, Kingship and Society,* Chicago, 1985.

———, *The Broken World of Sacrifice: An Essay in Ancient Indian Ritual,* Chicago, 1993.

Heidrum, Bruckner, Lothar Lutze, Aditya Malik (eds.), *Flags of Fame: Studies in South Asian Folk Culture,* Delhi, 1993.

Hiltebeitel, Alf, *The Cult of Draupadi: Mythologies: From Gingee to Kurukshetra,* Chicago, 1988.

———, *The Ritual of Battle: Krishna in the Mahābhārata,* Ithara, 1976.

———, (ed.), *Criminal Gods and Demon Devotees: Essays on the Guardians of Popular Hinduism,* Albany, 1989.

Herbert, A. Rosenfield, *Psychotic States: A Psychoanalytical Approach,* New York, 1965.

Huntington, Susan L. *The "Pala-Sena" Schools of Sculpture - Studies in South Asian Culture,* Ledien, 1984.

Inden, Ronald, "Hierarchies of Kings in Medieval India", *Contributions to Indian Sociology,* n.s. 15:99-125, 1981.

Isaac, Sequera, *Popular Culture - East and West,* Delhi, 1991.

Jamison, Stephaine, *Sacrificed Wife, Sacrificer's Wife; Women, Ritual and Hospitality in Ancient India,* New York., 1996.

Jayaseela, Stephen, *The Coromandel Coast and Its Hinterland: Economy, Society and Political System, 1500-1600,* New Delhi, 1991.

Jayasree, K., *Agrarian Economy in Andhra under Vijayanagar,* Delhi, 1991.

Jawaharlal, G., *Jainism in Andhra,* Hyderabad, 1994.

Jean, Baptist Tavernier., *Travel in India,* London, 1925.

Jean, Delloche, *Transport and Communications in India Prior to Steam Locomotion,* 2 Vols., Delhi, 1994.

Jha, D.N., *Feudal Social Formations in Early India,* Delhi, 1987.

———, *Economy and Society in Early India : Issues and Paradigms,* Delhi, 1993.

———, (ed.), *Feudal Social Formation in Early India,* Delhi, 1987.

———, (ed.), Society and Ideology in India (Essays in Honour of Professor R.S. Sharma), Delhi, 1996.

Kakar, Sudhir, *Inner World: A Psycho Analytic Study of Childhood and Society in India,* New Delhi, 1978.

———, *Shamans in India and its Healing Traditions,* Delhi, 1982.

———, *The Essential Writings of Sudhir Kakar,* Delhi, 2001.

Kamalakar (ed.), *Vishnu in Art, Thought and Literature,* Hyderabad, 1993.

Kane, P.V., *History of Dharmasastras,* Poona, 1974.

Kapadia, K.M., *Marriage and Family in India,* Bombay, 1958.

Karntz Frederich (ed.), *History from Below: Studies in Popular Protest and Popular Ideology,* Oxford, 1988.

Kesavan, Veluthat, *The Political Structure of Early Medieval South India,* Delhi, 1993.

Kinsely, David R., *Tantric Visions of the Divine Feminine,* Delhi, 1998.

———, *The Sword and the Flute: Kali and Krishna, Dark Visions of the Terrible and the Sublime in Hindu Mythology,* Berkely, 1975.

———, *Hindu Goddesses: Visions of the Divine Feminine in the Hindu Religious Tradition,* Delhi, 1987.

Kolenda, Pauline, "Women as Tribute, Women as Flower: Images of 'Women' in North and South India", *American Ethnologist*-11 : 98-117.

Krishna Kumari, M., *Studies in the History of Medieval Andhra,* Delhi, 1994.

———, *Facets of Andhra Culture,* Delhi, 1999.

———, *Sermons from Stones Contribution of Andhra to Art, Culture and Thought,* Delhi, 2002.

———, *Social and Cultural Life in Medieval Andhra,* Delhi, 1990.

———, *Pancharamas in Medieval Andhradesa,* Delhi, 1989.

———, (ed.), *Women as the Makers of History Proceedings of the Seminar,* Visakhapatnam, 2003.

———, (ed.), *Folklore Studies and its Bearing on History and Culture of Andhras, Proceedings of the Seminar*, Visakhapatnam, 2003.

Krishna Murty, K., *Social and Cultural Life in Ancient India,* Delhi, 1982.

Krishnamurty, Vaidehi A., *Social and Economic Conditions in Eastern Deccan*, Madras, 1970.

Krishna Swamy, Aiyangar, S., *Some Contributions of South India to Indian Culture,* Calcutta, 1923.

———, *Evolution of Hindu Administrative Institutions in South India,* Madras, 1931.

Kulke, Hermann., "A Passage to India: Temples, Merchants and the Ocean", *JESHO XXXVI,* May, 1993.

———, (ed.), *The State in India A.D. 1000-1700,* Delhi.

Kurtz, Stanley, *All the Mothers are one: Hindu India and the Cultural Reshaping of Psychoanalysis,* New York, 1992.

Lakshmi Narasamma, S., *Strila Patalu - Oka Parisilana,* Kakinada, 1989.

Lincoln, Bruce, *Death, War and Sacrifice; Studies in Ideology and Practice,* Chicago, 1991.

Lloyd, De Mause, *Foundations of Psychohistory,* New York, 1982.

———, (ed.), *The History of Childhood,* New York, 1974.

———, (ed.), *The New Psychohistory,* New York, 1975.

Lorenzen, David, N., "Warrior Ascetics in Indian History", *Journal of the American Oriental Society* 98:6-75, 1978.

Mahalingam, T.V., *Studies in the South Indian Temple Complex,* Dharwar, 1970.

———, *Administration and Social Life Under Vijayanagar,* Madras, New Delhi, 2nd ed., 1975.

Manu, *Dharma Sastra,* Trans. by George Buhler, Oxford, 1886.

Margabandhu, C., et. al., *Indian Archaeological Heritage (K.V. Soundara Rajan Felicitation Volume),* Delhi, 1991.

Maurice, Block and Jonathan Parry (eds.), *Death and the Regeneration of Life,* London, 1982.

McCrindle, *Ancient India as Described in Classical Literature,* 1901.

Meltzer, Donald, *The Psycho-Analytical Process,* London, 1967.

Milton, Rokeach, *Beliefs, Attitudes and Values: A Theory of Organization and Change,* London, 1968.

Mircea, Eliade, *Myths, Dreams and Mysteries - The Encounter Between Contemporary Faiths and Archaic Reality,* London, 1974.

Mishra, K.C., *The Cult of Jagannath,* Calcutta, 1971.

Misra T.N., *Impact of Tantra on Religion and Art,* Delhi, 1997.

Mitter, Partha, *Much Maligned Monsters - A History of European Reactions to Indian Art,* London, 1977.

Morag, Saich, *Discourse on Popular Culture: Class, Gender and History in Cultural Analysis, 1730 to the Present,* London, 1989.

Moreland, *Relations of Golconda,* London, 1931.

Nagaraja Rao, M.S. (ed.), *Kusumanjali - New Interpretations of Indian Art and Culture,* Delhi, 1989.

Nagasvami, R., "South Indian Temple as Employer", *The Indian Economic and Social History Review,* No. 4, 1965.

Nandi, R.N., *Religious Institutions and Cults in the Deccan A.D. 600-1000,* Delhi, 1973.

Nandi, Ramendra Nath, *State Formation, Agrarian Growth and Social Change in Feudal South India, A.D. 600-1200,* Delhi, 2000.

Narasimha Murty, A.V. & Suresh K.M. et. al., (eds) *Hemakuta - Recent Researchers in Archaeology and Museology (Shri CTM Kotraiah Felicitation Volume),* 2 vols. Delhi, 2001.

Narasemha Murty, A.V.N. and Sarma, I.K. (ed.), *Sri Ramachandrika (Prof Oruganti Ramachandraiya Festschrift) : Essays on Indian*

Archaeology, History, Epigraphy, Numismatics, Art and Religion, Delhi, 1993.

Narayanan, M.G.S., *Reinterpretations of South Indian History,* Trivandrum, 1977.

Narayana Rao, *Twentieth Century Telugu Poetry: An Anthology,* Delhi, 2002.

Narayana Rao, Velcheru & Shulman David (eds.), *Classical Telugu Poetry: An Anthology,* Delhi, 2002.

Noboru Karashima, *Indus Valley to Mekong Delta: Explorations in Epigraphy,* Madras, 1985.

———, *South Indian History and Society - Studies from Inscriptions A.D. 850-1800,* Delhi, 1984.

———, *Towards a New Formation - South Indian Society Under Vijayanagar Rule,* Delhi, 1992.

———, Subbarayalu, Y and Toru Matsui, *A Concordance of the Names in the Chola Inscriptions,* Madurai, 1978.

O Flaherty, Wendy Doniger, *The Origins of Evil in Hindu Mythology,* Berkeley, 1976.

———, *Women, Androgynes and other Mythical Beasts,* Chicago, 1980.

Ojha, Catherine, "Feminine Asceticism in Hinduism: Its Tradition and Present Condition", *Man in India* 61: 254-85, 1981.

Owen, M Lynched, *Divine Passions: The Social Construction of Emotion in India,* Berkeley, 1990.

Padma, A., *Socio-Cultural World of Women in Medieval Andhra,* Delhi, 2001.

Pal, Pratapaditya, *Hindu Religion and Iconology According to Tantrasāra,* Los Angels, 1981.

———, (ed.), *The Peaceful Liberators: Jain Art from India,* London.

Paul, B Courtright, *Ganesa - Lord of Obstacles, Lord of Beginning,* Oxford, 1985.

Peter, Burke, *Popular Culture in Early Modern Europe,* London, 1978.

Peter, Loewenberg, *Decoding the Past: The Psychohistorical Approach,* New York, 1983.

Preston, James J., *Cult of the Goddess: Social and Religious Change in a Hindu Temple,* New Delhi 1980.

Purchas, Samuel B.D., *Hakluyt Posthumous or Purchas, His Pilgrims,* Glasgow, 1905-1907.

Pushpendra Kumar, *Sakti Cult in Ancient India,* Varanasi, 1974.

Rajendra Prasad, B., *Art of South India: Andhra Pradesh,* Delhi, 1983.

———, *Temple Sculptures of Andhra Pradesh,* Hyderabad, 1978.

Raman K.V., Krishnan, K.G., et al. (eds.), *Srinidhi - Perspectives in Indian Archaeology, Art and Culture,* Madras, 1983.

Ramarao, M., *The Temples of Śrīśāilam,* Hyderabad, 1967.

———, *Śaivite Deities of Āndhradēśa,* Tirupati, 1966.

———, *Eastern Chālukyan Temples of Āndhradēśa,* Delhi, 1983.

Rama Rao, N.V.S., *Āndhra Sāhityamu - Sānghika Jivana Pratiphalanamu* (Telugu), Waltair, 1979.

Ramachandraiya, O., *Studies on Krishnadēvarāya of Vijayanagar,* Waltair, 1953.

Ramachandra Murty, S.S., *A Study of Telugu Place Names,* Delhi, 1985.

———, et al., (ed.), *Sānkaram : Recent Researches on Indian Culture,* Delhi, 2000.

Ramachandra Rao, C.V., *Administration and Society in Medieval Andhra, (A.D. 1038-1538) Under the Later Eastern Gangas and the Sūryavaṁśi Gajapatis,* Nellore, 1976.

Ramaraju, B., *Folklore of Andhra Pradesh,* Delhi, 1978.

———, *Āndhra Yōgulu,* Hyderabad, 1998.

Ramaswamy, Vijaya, *Textiles and Weavers in Medieval South India,* Delhi, 1985.

Rambhushan Prasad Singh, *Jainism in Early Medieval Karnataka,* Delhi, 1975.

Ramraj, *On the Studies of Indian Art*, Cambridge, 1983.

Rao, T.A.G., *Elements of Hindu Iconography,* 2 Vols., Varanasi, reprint, 1971.

Rawson, Ph., *Tantra Catalogue,* London Arts Council of Great Britain, 1971.

Reddi, G.N., *Poḍupu Kathalu,* Tirupati, 1988.

Richard, Shweder, *Thinking Through Cultures: Explorations in Cultural Psychology,* Cambridge, 1991.

Sahu, B.P. (ed.), *Land System and Rural Society in Early India - Readings in Early Indian History,* Delhi, 1997.

Saletore, B.A., *Social and Political Life in the Vijayanagar Empire (A.D. 1346-1646),* Vol. II, Madras, 1933.

Sankaranarayana, S., *Śrī Chakra,* Pondichery, 1970.

Saraswati, P., *Jānapada Sāhityamu - Pillala Pātalu,* Hyderabad, 1989.

Sarkar, Tanika and Urvasi Butalia (eds.), *Women and the Hindu Right: Collection of Essays, Kali for Women,* New Delhi, 1995.

Sarma I.K., Devraj D.V., and Gopal R (eds.), *Narasiṁhapriya - Essays on Indian Archaeology, Epigraphy, Numismatics, Art,*

Architecture, Iconography and Cultural History, New Delhi, 2000.

Sarma, M.S., *History of Reddi Kingdoms,* Visakhapatnam, 1948.

Saryu Prasad (ed.), *Tārā Rahasyam,* Varanasi, 1970.

Sastri, K.A.N., *Foreign Notices of South India from Megasthenes to Ma Huan,* Madras, 1939.

———, *Coḷas,* 2nd ed. Revised, Madras, 1975.

Sastri K.A.N. and Venkataramanayya, *Further Sources of Vijayanagar History,* 2 Vols, Madras, 1946.

Sastry, P.V.P., *The Kākatīyas of Warangal,* Hyderabad, 1978.

———, *Śrīśailam - Its History and Culture,* Hyderabad, 1982.

Satyanarayana, K., *A Study of the History and Culture of the Andhras,* 2 Vols., Delhi, 1983.

Sewell, Robert, *A Forgotten Empire (Vijayanagara) A Contribution to the History of India,* London, 1900.

Shamsastry, R. (ed.), *Kautilya's Arthaśāstra,* Mysore, 8th edition, 1967.

Shama R.C., *Mathura Museum and Art,* Delhi, 1975.

Sharma, R.S., *Survey of Research in Economic and Social History of India,* Delhi, 1986.

———, *Material Culture and Social Formations in Ancient India,* Delhi, 1983.

———, *Perspectives in Social and Economic History of Early India,* Delhi, 2nd edition, revised, 1995.

Sharma, R.S. and Jha D.N., *Indian Society: Historical Probings,* 2nd edition, Delhi, 1977.

Shulman, David Dean, *The Wisdom of Poets: Studies in Tamil, Telugu and Sanskrit,* Delhi, 2002.

———, *The Hungry God: Hindu Tales of Filicide and Devotion,* Chicago, 1993.

Singhi, N.K., Rajendra Joshi (eds.), *Religion, Ritual and Royalty,* Jaipur, 1999.

Sircar, D.C., *Studies in the Society and Administration of Ancient and Medieval India,* Vol. I, Calcutta, 1967.

Sivaramamurti, C., *The Art of India,* New York, 1977.

———, *Expressive Quality of Literary Flavour in Art,* New Series 6, Dharwar, 1974.

Soma Reddy, R., *Hindu and Muslim Religious Institutions of Andhradesa (A.D. 1300-1600)*, Madras, 1984.

Somasekhara Sarma M., *A Forgotten Chapter in Andhra History,* Waltair, 1948.

Sommerville, John C., "Towards a History of Childhood and Youth", *Journal of Interdisciplinary History*, 3 (1972), 438-47.

Spencer, George W., *The Politics of Expansion of Śrī Lanka and Śrī Vijaya,* Madras, 1983.

Srivatsava, Balarama, *Iconography of Sakti: A Study Based on Śrītattvanidhi,* Varanasi, 1978.

Stein, Burton, *Peasant, State and Society in Medieval South India,* Delhi, 1975.

———, (ed.), *South Indian Temples - An Analytical Reconstruction,* Delhi, 1975.

Subrahmanyam, Sanjay, "Aspects of State Formations - South India and Southeast Asia A.D. 1500-1650" in *Indian Economic and Social History Review,* 23, 4, 1986.

———, *Penumbral Visions: Making Politics in Early Modern South India,* Delhi, 2001.

———, *Political Economy and Commerce of Southrn India, A.D. 1500-1650,* Cambridge, 1990.

Sudersan, V., Prakasa Reddi, G & Suryanarayana, M. (eds.), *Religion and Society in South India,* Delhi, 1987.

Sundaram, K., *Studies in Economic and Social Conditions of Medieval Andhra,* Machilipatnam, 1968.

———, *The Siṁhāchalam Temple,* 2nd ed. Waltair, 1984.

Sundaram, R.V.S., *Andhrula Jānapada Vijñanamu,* Hyderabad, 1992.

Talbot, Cynthia, *Precolonial India in Practice: Society, Region and Identity in Medieval Andhra,* Delhi, 2001.

———, *Gifts to Gods and Brahmins: A Study of Religious Endowments in Medieval Andhra,* Ph.D. Dissertation, University of Wisconsin, Madison, 1988.

———, "Temples, Donors and Gifts: Patterns of Patronage in Thirteenth Century South India", *Journal of Asian Studies* 50 (2) pp. 308-40.

Tapper, Bruce E., "Widows and Goddesses: Female Roles in Deity Symbolism in a South Indian Village", *Contributions to Indian Sociology,* n.s. 13; 1-31, 1979.

———, *Rivalry and Tribute : Society and Ritual in a Telugu Village in South India.,* Delhi, 1987.

Thakore, S.R., *Catalogue of Sculptures in Archaeological Museum,* Gwalior.

Theodore, S. Hamerow, *Reflection on History and the Historians,* Madison, 1987.

Thurston Edgar, *Castes and Tribes of Southern India,* Reprint, Madras, 1975.

Vaidyanathan T.G. & Jeffrey J. Kripal (ed.), *Vishnu on Freud's Desk,* Delhi, 1999.

Van der Hock (ed.), *Ritual, State and History in South Asia, Essays in Honour of Heesterman,* London, 1992.

Vasudevan C.S., *Temples of Andhra Pradesh,* Delhi, 2000.

Venkataramanayya, N., *Studies in the History of the Third Dynasty of Vijayanagar Empire,* Madras, 1935.

———, *An Essay on the Origin of the South Indian Temple,* Madras, 1930.

Venkataratnam, A.V., *Local Government in the Vijayanagar Empire,* Mysore, 1972.

Vankooij, Karel R., *Worship of the Goddess according to the Kalikapurana,* Leiden, 1972.

Vankooj Houben & Karel R Vankooj (ed.), *Violence, Denied Violence, Non-Violence and the Rationalisation of Violence,* Leiden, 1999.

Waghorne Joanne P. and Norman Cutler (eds.), *Gods of Flesh, Gods of Stone: The Embodiment of Divinity in India,* Chambersburg.

Yvonne, Y Haddad and Ellison B Findly, (eds.), *Women, Religion and Social Change,* Albany, 1985.

Yazdani, G., *Early History of Deccan,* Oxford University Press, 1960.

Ziegendbalg, B., *Geneology of the South Indian Gods: A Manual of the Mythology and Religion of the People of South India,* Delhi, 2000.

Zimmer, Heinrich, *The Art of Indian Asia: Its Mythology and Transformation,* 2 Vols., New York, 1955.

———, *Myths and Symbols in Indian Art and Civilization,* New York, 1962.

INDEX

❑❑❑

I A: Mother and child-From Madhya Pradesh; Five grahaṣ above, Gaṇēśa and devotees

I B: Mother and child, Rajshahi Dist. Pala School, 11th century A.D., National Museum, Delhi-Navagrahas, Śivalinga above, dancers and musicians below

I C: Mother and child-Central India-Navagrahas, Gaṇēśa and Śiva liṅga above

II A: Śrī Chakra Temple, Devipuram, Vishakapatnam District (A.P.) - General view

II B: Śrī Chakra Temple - elevation of the temple

III: Gaṇēśa, British Museum, London

IV A: Ādivarāha, Ashmolean Museum, Oxford-View from right side

IV B: Ādivarāha, Ashmolean Museum, Oxford-View from left side

V A: Pārśvanātha, Victoria & Albert Museum, London

V B: Śāntinātha, Victoria & Albert Museum, London

V C: Mahāvīra image on Sangamayya Konda, Kollivalasa, Srikakulam District (A.P.)

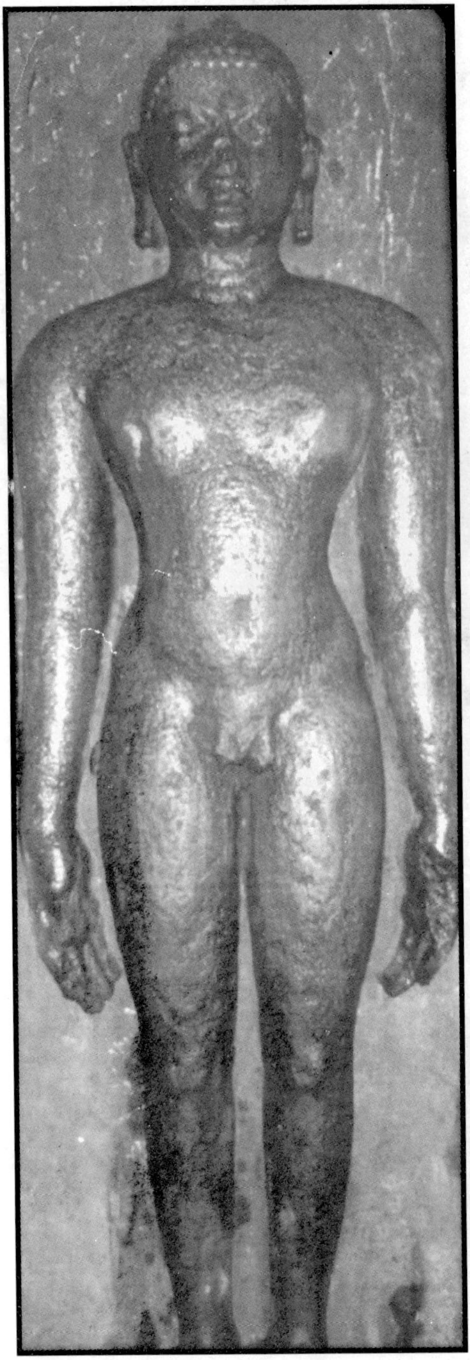

V D: Jain Tīrthāṅkara in the sanctum of Sangamayya Konda, Srikakulam District (A.P.)